Danci

"In *Dancing with My Father*, we learn along with Sally Clarkson how to experience peace and joy through all the challenges life has to offer. The scripture offered and questions asked at the end of each chapter make this a wonderful book for individual or group study."

—BRENDA NULAND, homeschooling mom and blogger,
found at http://coffeeteabooksandme.blogspot.com

"Sally Clarkson's warmth and wisdom remind us to quit worrying about our footwork, lean into God's embrace, and let Him lead in this joy-filled dance called life!"

—LISA HARPER, popular speaker and author of *A Perfect Mess*

"Ever long for a gentle, godly mentor? One who with words and by example, graciously guides you through the maze of life, encouraging you to see with your heart, hear with your soul, and ultimately discover God in the midst of it all? You hold in your hands a mentoring manual creatively crafted by Sally Clarkson. This treasure will enable you to confidently rise above the circumstances of your life, unearthing contentment and calm as you too learn to delightfully dance with your heavenly Father."

—KAREN EHMAN, national speaker for Proverbs 31 Ministries
and author of *A Life That Says Welcome* and *The Complete
Guide to Getting and Staying Organized*

"With grace, candor, and engaging true-life stories, Sally Clarkson helps readers rediscover the reality of enduring joy in a fallen world. This is a book well worth reading!"

—CHERI FULLER, speaker and author of *Mother-Daughter Duet*

"This is not another 'don't worry, be happy' book. Sally gets to the heart of what true joy looks like and how to hold on to it through *all* circumstances of life. I highly recommend this book—and Sally Clarkson!"

—GINGER KOLBABA, former editor of *Today's Christian Woman* magazine, founding editor of Kyria.com, and author of the novel *Desperate Pastors' Wives*

"A breath of fresh air for weary travelers on the ministry road. With characteristic grace and wisdom, Sally Clarkson acknowledges that even the most devoted Christian suffers discouragement, disappointment, and disillusionment. She meets us in our crashed idealism and burnout—but she doesn't leave us there. With God at her side, she leads us to the gentle peace and quiet trust of a mature Christian. I've read all of Sally's books; this work is her best yet!"

—ELIZABETH FOSS, mother of nine and author of *Real Learning: Education in the Heart of the Home*

"These pages sing a song that could change your life. In lyrical prose that truly captivates, in the rhythm of personal narrative and startling truth, *Dancing with My Father* invites the soul-hungry, the joy-lame, and the spirit-weary to come to the soiree and stay. This isn't another paint-by-number, formulaic book, but an honest, thoughtful invitation to live an authentic life of biblical joy."

—ANN VOSKAMP, columnist for ChristianWomenOnline.net and the *San Antonio Christian Beacon*, and a blogger, found at www.aholyexperience.com

"As you turn these pages, your precious Father God will twirl you into a dance of joy with Him!"

—LINDA DILLOW, author of *Calm My Anxious Heart* and coauthor of *Intimate Issues*

Dancing *with* My Father

How God Leads Us into a Life
of Grace and Joy

Dancing *with* My Father

SALLY CLARKSON

Author of *The Mission of Motherhood*.

WaterBrook
PRESS

DANCING WITH MY FATHER
PUBLISHED BY WATERBROOK PRESS
12265 Oracle Boulevard, Suite 200
Colorado Springs, Colorado 80921

All Scripture quotations, unless otherwise indicated, are taken from the New American Standard Bible®. © Copyright The Lockman Foundation 1960, 1962, 1963, 1968, 1971, 1972, 1973, 1975, 1977, 1995. Used by permission. (www.Lockman.org). Scripture quotations marked (NIV) are taken from the Holy Bible, New International Version®. NIV®. Copyright © 1973, 1978, 1984 by International Bible Society. Used by permission of Zondervan Publishing House. All rights reserved. Scripture quotations marked (KJV) are taken from the King James Version.

Italics in Scripture quotations reflect the author's added emphasis.

ISBN 978-0-307-45706-6
ISBN 978-0-307-45851-3 (electronic)

Published in the United States by WaterBrook Multnomah, an imprint of the Crown Publishing Group, a division of Random House Inc., New York.

WATERBROOK and its deer colophon are registered trademarks of Random House Inc.

Library of Congress Cataloging-in-Publication Data
Clarkson, Sally.
    Dancing with my father : how God leads us into a life of grace and joy / Sally Clarkson.—1st ed.
        p. cm.
    ISBN 978-0-307-45706-6—ISBN 978-0-307-45851-3 (electronic) 1. Christian women—
Religious life. 2. Joy—Religious aspects—Christianity. 3. Clarkson, Sally. I. Title.
    BV4527.C565 2010
    248.8'43—dc22

                                        2009035854

Printed in the United States of America
2011

10 9 8 7 6 5 4 3 2

SPECIAL SALES
Most WaterBrook Multnomah books are available at special quantity discounts when purchased in bulk by corporations, organizations, and special-interest groups. Custom imprinting or excerpting can also be done to fit special needs. For information, please e-mail SpecialMarkets@WaterBrookMultnomah.com or call 1-800-603-7051.

I dedicate this to my wonderful father,
John Bone, my first dance partner.
Thanks for modeling a life of joy.

Contents

One

The Search for Joy in a Less-Than-Perfect World

Monday morning was here again. I opened my eyes reluctantly, since snuggling under my warm covers on this snowy, Colorado spring day seemed more desirable than facing the responsibilities that shouted for my attention. Marriage. Parenting. Church. Work. Extended family. Friends. Everyone and everything seemed to need me, constantly wanting more and more of my time and attention, leaving little for me and my passions and interests.

After twenty-eight years of marriage and twenty-five years of parenting, I was accustomed to these burdens that sometimes weighed heavily on my shoulders. As I lay in bed, I compiled a mental list of what was ahead of me in my day. Making breakfast for two of my children who were still at home; finishing the dishes from last night's dinner party; attacking the piles of laundry that had accumulated over the last busy week; facing the deadline on a freelance project that still wasn't finished; helping my daughter with her history report; discussing with my husband how to deal with our sons' college bills and the need to replace the tires on our older car...

On and on the list grew until I wanted to pull the covers over my head and stay in bed. I was already weary of the work ahead, and the day had not even begun!

In the midst of this, my fourteen-year-old daughter came into my bedroom with tears in her eyes. "Mom, do you remember my friend from church who's been battling a brain tumor?"

"Yes," I told her. I remembered him well. My daughter and I had prayed often for his healing.

"I just got an e-mail that he died this morning. I don't get it. We prayed so hard!"

"I know," I said, hugging her to me.

"I just feel so empty."

We talked and prayed, and I was struck again by thoughts that had captivated my attention for almost a year. With so much sadness and so many daily burdens to shoulder, how do Christian women maneuver steadily through this journey of life with joy and peace of heart intact? What does it look like to be a woman filled with joy, every day, all the time, no matter what? In the deluge of all the stresses and disappointments in a fallen world, how does a mature Christian woman really walk in the power of the Holy Spirit? How does she face each situation with gladness, despite the relentless and demanding day-after-day, month-after-month, year-after-year things that would rob her of emotional and creative energy, such as chores, bills, arguments, messes? Or how does she maintain joy in the center of more devastating troubles: a divorce, the tragic death of a loved one, a child who has a chronic illness or disability, rejection by family members, alcoholism and drug-related scars, a job layoff?

For me, the times I struggle most to experience joy are when I feel an invisible finger pointing at my heart, accusing me of all my inadequacies: *How can you be a Christian this long and still lose your temper or struggle with pettiness, entertain critical attitudes, fluctuate in your emotions and in your walk with the Lord?* Guilt over disappointing God or others sometimes lurks in the recesses of my mind and hovers silently like a cloud over my subconscious soul. After all, I have been a Christian for many years and am perceived as a mature leader, writer, and speaker; shouldn't I be able to conquer these obstacles with confidence and strength? Shouldn't joy be as natural to me as breathing?

PONDERING IN POLAND

My daughter went back to her room to get ready for school. Slowly I got out of bed and moved to the kitchen to brew some tea. As I looked out the kitchen window, I thought back to a similar spring morning, almost exactly one year before, when I first began to wrestle with this issue. That particular April morning found me sitting on a park bench outside the old city gates of Krakow, Poland, my last stop on a mission trip. Many years before when I was a young missionary, Krakow was where I grew into my idealism about life and faith. This was the place where I began to live passionately for the Lord, where I determined to walk each day with my hand in his.

Now I had returned to Poland, still idealistic in my heart, but a weary, life-worn, older Christian looking for spiritual equilibrium. Returning to a place that held such wonderful spiritual memories provided a good opportunity for me to reevaluate my life, to take inventory of my spiritual resources, and to judge whether I needed any midcourse correction.

Before arriving in Poland, my mission trip had led me through five countries and numerous encounters with groups, leaders, and individuals. Although I know it might sound adventurous and exciting, my packed schedule of meetings and speaking engagements, over a period of three weeks, traveling on planes and trains, sleeping in all sorts of beds, and eating a variety of unfamiliar foods was physically and emotionally taxing. But even with the physical demands, I found that my body was not nearly as weary as my spirit.

On this trip, I conversed with countless people—many who were committed to Christ, and some who had been leaders and missionaries for many years. Spending time with them put me on spiritual battlegrounds where many of these devoted had been injured. I took their burdens into my own life. As I listened to person after person share their depression and soul battles, their temptation to give up on ideals, and how they each sought to keep their heads above the waters of despair, I realized I needed their mirror to look into my own soul.

I wanted to live freely and celebrate the joy that God promised as a fruit of his Spirit, and to live it out in the midst of a less-than-perfect world that challenges my faith and Christian paradigm every day. Having lived as a spiritually committed person for many years, I saw that my soul had slowly been drained by taxing relationships and circumstances, the mysteries of life that cultivate doubt, and a culture that fosters cynicism. I had battled through depression several times while enduring bitter trials and deep hurts at the hands of others, mostly Christians. Facing all these difficulties had, at times, left me fearful of life. When I had struggled through so many life-wars in my past, how could I face what was ahead without fear or doubt in God's ability to do something, especially when often he seemed silent and unaware of my needs?

I sat on the park bench in Poland wondering how my friends and I had become fragile, discouraged, and vulnerable, bearing the hurts and burdens of life. *Is it even possible to live as a joyful Christian in this fallen world?* I asked myself. *Do I really know what it means to live a victorious Christian life?* Scripture seemed to promise power, happiness, the fruit of the Spirit, and unconditional love amongst believers. But that was not always my normal experience, and apparently it was not the normal experience of the many Christians and missionaries I met throughout the years.

As I sat and pondered, I realized that I didn't really *believe* any differently than I had so many years ago when I was fresh and young and innocent. My journey began by holding God's hand, and I knew that I was still holding on. Yet I could see that somewhere along the way, I had become less confident that I even knew what it meant to walk hand in hand with him. My sense of security in my relationship with him had been gradually worn down by the scars and injuries of daily life. My head told me that God was still there, offering the promises he'd always held out to me. But my heart struggled to find assurance.

Help me, I prayed. And that small park, in the midst of obscurity where no one knew my whereabouts, became a sanctuary in which I met, once again, with God.

Memories flooded my mind as I thought about the familiar haunts of my youth, some thirty years before when I started out as a missionary in this country. In order to live "freely" in Poland, my friend Gwen and I enrolled in the Jagiellonian University as students. But in reality, that was our cover; we were there to take the sweet message of Christ to this country that had been overwhelmed by communism.

I traveled through communist Eastern Europe, when Christianity was forbidden to be practiced, taking messages to secret Christian contacts in Poland, Romania, Czechoslovakia, Yugoslavia, and Hungary and meeting with people to teach them the Word of God. These were the days when I cut my spiritual teeth, gathering with people who were hungry and excited to receive the message of God's love.

A deep happiness and joy had energized those days, as I sensed that I was part of a strategic work for the kingdom of God. I experienced heartfelt satisfaction because I confidently believed I was God's hands and voice to people who were so responsive to the simple messages of his

love and redemption. Innocence and idealism ruled authoritatively in
those days when hope and childlike faith protected my heart from the
despair of life in a fallen world. Joy fed my soul daily as I saw many people respond to our sincere messages. Miracles were an expected order of
my day, when prayers for God's help and leading were offered with unwa-
vering confidence.

A Child's Dance

There in the park I remembered the good feelings of that time when life
felt exciting and all dreams were possibilities. It dawned on me that I had
felt this excitement at other times in my life: when I was engaged to be
married, pregnant with my first child, starting our first church job, moving into missions with my husband and children. Each anticipated
change brought a surge of expectation and confidence that good things
lay ahead, an assurance that my life held the hope of goodness and joy and
satisfaction. All these positive feelings were fueled by dreams of what I
thought life could hold. Often my dreams had not reflected the reality of
the burdens and responsibilities that such life decisions would entail. As
a young woman, I hadn't yet even understood the costs of living life ide-
alistically in a fallen world.

What had changed? What had shifted my heart from the passion
and excitement of childlike faith to weary plodding, faithfully putting
my foot down one step at a time while feeling the heaviness of life on my
shoulders? I had let my burdens weigh me down and throw a shadow
over my thoughts and emotions. As I grew older, hope and excitement
at the prospect of a new adventure in marriage, parenting, work, or
church were often replaced with disappointment and disillusionment.

I sat on that park bench and found myself longing for the energy,
hope, and joy of the earlier days when I had begun this journey. Realiza-

tion dawned upon my heart: I didn't want to live as a victim—cynical, depressed, and overwhelmed by the load that so many carried. I wanted that childlike innocence that believed in the goodness of God.

Not wanting my circumstances to determine my attitude toward life and my spiritual stability, I prayed, *Lord, please show me how to maintain joy, to cultivate an inner peace and delight, a strength that will support me through sadness and difficulty. Help me to end my life well, to still be as resilient as I was when you first called me to be yours. Let me find you and your reality anew.*

At that moment, my eyes were drawn to a little boy, twirling and dancing in circles. He held his hands high above his head, grasping at tree blossoms falling gently like snowflakes in the soft breeze. His chubby toddler face was full of delight. Obviously unencumbered and totally unselfconscious, he giggled each time he caught a falling blossom.

That is how I want to be, I realized. I wanted to be as a child, delighting in life, at peace with God, living in the grace of the moment. I wanted to live above the pull of depression and cultivate a heart of joy from which others could draw. I wanted to learn what it really meant to be filled with the reality of God, the love of God, and the joy of God every day, no matter what else was going on in my life.

I knew I stood at a crossroad that would determine what kind of a Christian I would be from that point forward: victorious, lighthearted, and free—or downcast, weighed down, and wounded. I realized that I didn't want to cross the finish line of life gasping for spiritual breath, clenching my teeth as I wearily crossed into the presence of God. Although I didn't want to be a Pollyanna, pretending away sadness, pain, and difficulty and denying the real grieving that comes with loss and disappointment, I did want to find the good in all things, to experience the reality of God's joy anew right in the middle of my trials and stresses.

And so began a spiritual journey, a search for biblical joy, the kind that satisfies deeply, that brings hope through tears, love when wronged, and peace that passes understanding.

My Dance with My Father

Now here I was, one year after my crossroads decision on that park bench, sipping tea while thoughts of my menial daily tasks, my daughter's friend's passing, and the memories of my prayer in Poland mingled in my mind. As I settled into my quiet-time chair, a blue Queen Anne chair close to my bed, another memory came, this one from almost fifty years before. As I remembered the little boy twirling and dancing in the park, it was as though the Holy Spirit directed me to a long-ago image that he wanted me to have—that of dancing with my father.

My sweet father was a bigger-than-life figure to me when I was a little girl. Standing at six feet three in his stocking feet, he was a slim, towering figure, always poking or patting someone. He was an extrovert's extrovert, full of life and constantly making friends wherever he went. He was always bright and smiling, kind of a song-and-dance man—whistling, singing, or humming, with a wink and a wiggle as he danced his way through life. His friends in college called him "Slick," a nickname that stuck because he was, for his time, the epitome of "cool." Although he was naturally outgoing, I think part of his personality was also shaped from growing up as a Depression child, surrounded by much sadness. As an adult, he seemed determined to live with as little acknowledgment of sadness as possible, to work hard to provide for his family, and to give us opportunities to enjoy the pleasures of life that his own parents had not been able to afford.

I loved my father, and I know he loved me and my brothers. And yet, probably like other children of my generation, I didn't receive a lot of personal, one-on-one time with him. He worked long hours to provide for my mother, two older brothers, and me. Although ours was a secure home, filled with lots of family time and people, time *alone* with my dad—just him and me—was rare, and so precious and treasured.

I used to write stories about him and was thrilled when he gave me any sort of special attention, kissed my cheek, or spoke a personal word of love or affirmation.

One vibrant summer evening, when the sweet scents of roses and honeysuckle from our yard were carried along on the breezes of the night, my parents allowed me to attend an adult party with them. While it was a social affair of some sort that was just one of many for them, it was an auspicious occasion for a little girl of eight. I am not sure why I was allowed to attend the party with them; there must have been no baby-sitter available and no brothers at home that night. Even all these years later, I still clearly remember getting ready for the great affair with the help of my mother, who always made grand preparations for special events.

As I watched, she donned a sleek royal blue chiffon dress with a swirling skirt that begged for movement. Large rhinestone drops were mounted on her earlobes, and a sparkling matching necklace framed and accentuated her lovely features. She added two circles of rouge on her high cheekbones and ruby red lipstick to her lips.

"You look like a princess!" I told her in awe. The final spray of cologne made her smell like one too.

"Now it's time to make *you* into a princess," she said to me with a playful voice. And at that, she lifted me up, placed me gently on her bathroom vanity, and added some never-before-experienced magic to my face! A little rouge, some hand lotion rubbed gently on my rough little-girl hands, a squirt of her very own perfume, and I began to feel more and more like a little princess. I remember dressing in a sky blue polished-cotton dress adorned with delicate eyelet lace and belted with a satin sash. Surely, my mother and I would be the most beautiful girls at the party.

My father lifted me into their car. I was perched on top of the elevated middle armrest, which served as my own special cushioned seat between my sophisticated parents. (This was before the days when seat belts and car seats would interfere with a little girl's delight of riding in style.) My father dropped my mother and me off at the front door of the country club where the party was being held. A tall, elegantly dressed doorman clad in black opened our car door and ushered us into the foyer, which opened into a large ballroom. The room was a whirl of pleasures to delight the senses, glimmering with sparkling lights, candles, and flowers, while a Glenn Milleresque big band was pounding out rhythms and filling the room with the sounds of horns.

We were seated at a round table laden with silver, china, crystal, and thick linen napkins, all adding to the sparkle, gleam, and splendor of the night. My wide blue eyes took in the lavish celebration. It was such a delight to my young, unsophisticated senses and seemed like a kind of fantasy world. The dance floor filled with couples, twirling and swaying to the music. I sat at our table and excitedly took it all in. But the longer I watched all the festivity, the more I longed for a chance to be a participant instead of just an onlooker.

It seemed to me that my black, shiny patent-leather shoes were made for tapping and dancing on the floor among all the jewel-bedecked, rouge-faced women swirling and laughing with their husbands. Visions of romance marched through the corridors of my girlish mind as I dreamed of a future day when I would be on the arm of my very own partner, gracefully and lightly gliding over the floor. An involuntary surge of excitement and joy at being caught up in the pulsing rhythms bubbled up from some hidden corner of my being. I stood and began to sway to the melodies, tapping my toes to the rhythms of the band, lost in the wonder of the moment.

Suddenly, my handsome, smiling father strolled over. In one easy, graceful movement, he swept me off my feet and up into his arms. With a tone and look of noble seriousness, he said, "May I have a dance with the princess of the ball?"

"Yes," I said with my little girl smile. The next thing I knew we were on the dance floor. My feet hung limply down, swinging as he swayed. He held me tightly in his strong arms and easily twirled me 'round and 'round the dance floor. As we danced cheek to cheek, I breathed in the familiar scent of the Old Spice aftershave he had lightly rubbed on his smooth-shaven face earlier that evening. (That spicy aroma still brings back memories of him.) The tingling excitement and pride that I felt at that giddy moment, being in the arms of my hero, left me almost breathless. I treasured each second with great delight and took in all the smiles and admiration of the other doting adults. For the several minutes we were on the dance floor, I was caught up in something so special I didn't want it to end.

But then the song wound to a close, and the music came to an abrupt stop. Our dance was over. With his long, smooth strides, my father glided back to our dinner table with me still in his arms and set me lightly upon my chair.

"Thank you for the pleasure of your company, sweet princess," he said affectionately and bowed. Then he turned away to find my mother.

I hadn't visited this lovely memory in many years, but even as I thought of it again that Monday morning, it brought a smile to my lips. My father was always my hero; I longed for his love, and I cherished his attention and affection, as any girl does.

Though he passed away more than fifteen years ago, just to think about him brings me pleasure—his antics, his exuberant spirit, the affectionate kisses and embraces he gave to my mom as he walked through a room, the times I remember him telling me I was pretty, rare though they were. His wonderful mixture of many qualities gives me pleasure to know that this man was my father.

I smiled as the memories allowed me to reexperience the delight of that night with my parents, feeling the intimacy of their focused attention and remembering the magical ambiance of the evening when I drank in the romance and enjoyed the rhythms of the music and of life.

On with the dance! Let joy be unconfined...

LORD BYRON

A PICTURE OF WHAT GOD WANTS

Now almost fifty years later, my Monday morning thoughts flooded me anew with the reminder that I wanted to live my life and build my attitudes on those truths that give life to my heart and expression to my desire to embrace beauty and goodness. I renewed my decision, made in Poland, that joy would be my goal, that I would look everywhere I go for God's touch, his shadow, his signature. I would celebrate the inner reality of his Spirit, rather than live as a victim of circumstances in my outward reality.

That morning, in the midst of the mundane to-do list and the tragic news, I rededicated this whole area to the Lord. I told him that I wanted to reflect his character and reality, that I wanted to love him and be filled every day with his joy, so that others who see me would have a glimpse of God—in my words, in my affection, in my writing, in disappointments and trials, and even in my everyday tasks. I longed for him to "restore to me the joy" of his salvation (Psalm 51:12).

The memory of dancing with my father provided a picture of what God desires for *us* to share. He gave me a personal, visual image of what he wanted me to understand about his joy: that it is wrapped up in him as my heavenly Father, that he is the Initiator, the Provider, the Lover, the Strong One. In short, he is to be my leading man in the dance of life.

But even more, dancing seemed to be a visual picture of what God wants me to do in my soul: he wants me to dance inside my heart, no matter what is going on outside in my circumstances. To dance is to celebrate life, to make merry, to physically live out the reality of internal joy. Those who walk closely with the Lord have a secret inner joy, a dancing energy just from knowing him. It is in having him as my partner, in letting him take the lead, that I will be directed around the "dance floor" of my life. He is the One who will show me the steps, how to listen to the music, how to engage my heart with him and to stay in sync with him, the real Source of the music, the dance, and the everlasting joy.

Where would this fit into my reality? I had to put my finger on what had placed a cloud of darkness over my thoughts and feelings so that I could know practically how to reconcile, on a moment-to-moment basis, the distance between the outer world I lived in and the inner world of his presence, the place I desired to dwell.

I MADE THE DECISION

To strengthen my commitment to make joy my goal, I started a blog called I Take Joy at www.itakejoy.com. There I wrote about my desire to dance through my life with his joy, to seek to be resilient, and to learn to celebrate every day the present reality of living face to face with the Lord.

In response to my writing, I received letters from women all over the world who share in this desire:

"I want to find joy every day."

"I am committed to the same thing."

"I decided not to be a victim of my circumstances, so I have committed to living a life with joy at the center."

Through this process I have learned that, to use an old cliché, the journey of joy begins with a single step. We step in the direction of the Lord and say, "Walk this pathway with me anew. Hold my hand. Show me how to live the way you designed me to live in the first place." Those I found along this same path agreed that in order to regularly experience the joy of the Lord, we must make a focused decision.

"Do not be deceived, God is not mocked; for whatever a man sows, this he will also reap," I read in Galatians 6:7. If I was going to find the joy of walking with God minute by minute, it would take a personal commitment from me to choose joy, to seek joy, to invest in joy, to "sow" joy into my life in ways that are biblical and true. So in my quiet-time place, as I talked about all of this to my heavenly Father, I planted a flag of faith. I prayed, "From this day on, I will choose to cultivate joy and to pursue it in your presence, so that I may indeed walk in the reality of the fruit of God's Spirit reflecting joy through me—every day, no matter what."

As the weeks passed, I assessed my life in light of my new goal. And in that assessment I found some obstacles that had kept me from experiencing what I knew God said, through Scripture, is possible to have.

One of the greatest obstacles was my response to disappointments, frustration, and the day-to-day interruptions of life. As I evaluated these things in light of my commitment to walk in joy, I could see that, in reality, God had used many of my difficulties to create in me a deeper, more compassionate heart. I could see that the hand of God had faithfully met me at my need and somehow sustained me instead of letting me go under. I also realized that he had used these challenges to loosen my grip on the worldly, temporal things I had previously looked to for security and stability and instead compelled me to rely on him and seek eternal answers.

I have never relished the thought of more suffering! But I knew that such times created a deeper hunger in my soul for spiritual realities and answers that satisfied the deep places in my heart. Something in me longed for more—more loving intimacy with others, more deep pleasure in the moments of my life. There was also deep longing for beauty and adventure. I wanted to know that my life was made to be meaningful, that my God was with me always! I even hoped for innocence and a pure, childlike heart in a sophisticated, cynical, fatalistic world. And so I committed this area into God's hands and looked for the shadows of his reality in my world, learning to expect his answers, to hear from him in the moments of my life.

It took work and prayer, but that commitment to my desire *continues* to pay great rewards.

Committing to this ideal has led me to more joy. I'm reminded of the pearl merchant who searched all over the world for a pearl of great value, and when he found it, he sold all that he had to own it.

When we change the focus of our heart, we will begin to find answers. The commitment leads in the direction of the fulfillment. We are not to look for temporal happiness, to have our own way; instead we are to look for the true, authentic joy that comes from God, the Source of joy.

You may be where I was not so very long ago, wondering how to have a joy-filled Christian life and whether it is even possible. You may be at a place in your life that is mundane and routine, and so you are looking for a return of your spiritual passion. Or perhaps you find yourself in the midst of tragedy and need reassurance that joy is still possible. Maybe you long for the knowledge that God has something more for you—not a Pollyannaish sense of happiness but something real that can guide and shape your life.

I pray that by picking up this book, you will begin to take the steps that will lead you closer to God and that you will soon find yourself twirling in the joy of dancing with the Father.

> You have turned for me my mourning into dancing;
> you have loosed my sackcloth and girded me with
> gladness, that my soul may sing praise to You and not be
> silent. O LORD my God, I will give thanks to You forever.
>
> PSALM 30:11–12

Finding *Your* Rhythm in God's Joy

Perhaps as you read this book, surveying your life will lead you to answer the questions, needs, and desires you have for finding joy—in all circumstances, at all times. As you ponder what God desires for you and as you look at the joy that may be missing from your life, ask yourself these questions:

1. What hinders me from "feeling his joy"?

2. What is the most prominent feeling about life that I have? Where did it come from?

    Doing for others – helping to make things — certain jobs abilities that God has given me

3. What is my greatest area of disillusionment or the circumstance that most often robs me of joy?

Criticism

4. What do my attitudes say about God's character? Are there any areas in which I have subtly believed that God is not concerned about my personal needs? What are the unanswered prayers in my life that I am still waiting for him to answer?

Writing down the answers to these questions in a journal helped me evaluate what I needed to understand and how I needed to begin making better choices. Journaling helped me see that God faithfully leads and teaches us his steps. I encourage you to record what he speaks to your heart as you join me on the journey into joy.

Dear heavenly Father,

Please move in my heart. Teach me to live in the fullness of your joy. Show me through your Word and by your Holy Spirit how I might learn to dance my life with you as my lead, following your steps, listening to the rhythm of your love. Take my burdens into your hands and lighten my load as I seek you in the deep places of my heart. Amen.

Two

A Heart That Dances to Celebrate God's Presence

At eleven years old, my second son, Nathan, was wiggly, loud, extroverted, and all boy. But on Christmas Eve afternoon, as I was fussing with all the food, gift wrapping, and Christmas tasks that needed to be tended to, he asked to "please, please" meet with me alone. I was up to my elbows in bread dough and busy mentally checking off my to-do list. Yet something in my heart told me this rare request was an important moment, so I decided to make time for this mysterious meeting.

I followed him into my bedroom.

"Close the door, please," he said. I noticed he was gingerly hiding something beneath his jacket. I did as he requested. "Sit down, Mom. This is important."

Perplexed by this serious encounter with my normally laughing child, I sat down, wondering what trouble he might have caused. But as Nathan turned to face me, his entire countenance was shining with delight. He pulled a single long-stem red rose out from under his jacket.

"I wanted to give you this because I wanted you to know how much I love you before you gave me Christmas presents tomorrow. I made

Daddy drive me to the store. I love you, Mom. You're the best. Merry Christmas."

He quickly kissed me and wrapped me in a bear hug to seal the deal.

This love gift took me totally by surprise. His offering was more meaningful than any other Christmas present I would receive. All of my children often told me that they loved me. But Nathan didn't want to just say the words. He wanted to demonstrate his love by doing something exceptional, by giving me a gift to acknowledge my worth in his eyes. He wanted to give to me in a manner like that he felt he had been given to!

As a parent, I had been thinking all day long about how to make my children's Christmas special, how to serve them. And yet here was a love offering from the heart of one of the precious ones I had already decided to bless. His gift, like mine, involved thoughtfulness and advance planning. He was providing me with a deep sense of appreciation and love. He gave from a pure heart, out of spontaneous affection and a desire to bless me. His gift was sealed with a smacking kiss on my cheek and a wraparound hug.

As I sat next to this beloved bundle on my bedroom couch, I tried to tell him just how much his gift meant to me. "You know, Nathan, you are one of a kind. It was very considerate of you to think of me and then to go to the trouble of buying a beautiful gift for me, knowing it would bring me pleasure. I really appreciate that you didn't just tell me in words but you gave your love to me in a thoughtful deed. You know, you remind me of my Bible hero, David. He was different from all of the other Israelites in his time. He had such a big heart, and he was always looking for ways to give his love back to God. I think you will be a great leader like him someday."

"Mama, tell me again about David with a different heart! I want to be like him."

And so my little couch became a time-traveling vehicle, taking us from the present into the story Nathan had heard so many times before, the story that I too had loved hearing as a child.

A SHOW OF LOVE AND FAITH

Our oversize family Bible seemed an auspicious book to me as a little girl. It was preserved in the living room, where all valuable relics were held. I would sneak reverently and quietly into this adult room, take it off the coffee table, and ceremoniously have my own "Bible time." I loved looking at the glossy classical art pages in the middle of the book. I was impressed with the vibrantly colored dramatic renditions of the most famous Bible stories. My favorite pictures were of David.

In one, he was dressed in a flowing, short orange tunic that looked like a lady's swirly skirt. He stood next to a gnarled olive tree, casting a defiant glance at a gigantic man glaring back with hatred. In my mind, I saw saliva dripping from the jeering mouth of Goliath. (Nathan always giggled when he heard this!)

Goliath seemed to be a cross between a monster and an ogre. David wielded a slingshot, much like the squirrel-hunting slingshot Uncle Frank used to amuse my brothers. With a harplike instrument hanging off a leather strap on his back, David had the slingshot pulled back to its full extent, aimed directly at the giant before him.

My mother would occasionally dramatize the story of David and Goliath for me, as I squished against her to look at the pictures while she told me the story: "There was a terrible giant who was an enemy of God. And every day he and thousands of his best trained soldiers would gather on the hills of Israel to fight against the Israelites. He shouted and challenged the Israelites to send a brave man to fight against him. Whoever won would take the victory for his nation. Day after day, the bravest soldiers of Israel would gather to see if there was a single man courageous enough to fight against the giant. But day after day, no one could be found because the giant was bigger and stronger than anyone, and all the soldiers knew that any among their men would be killed instantly.

"But there was a boy named David who had a *different heart*. His heart was brave and strong because he believed that his God could help him do anything. God had helped him kill a bear when he was out in the meadow tending sheep. He had also helped him kill a lion. He helped David practice being brave. When David brought food to his brothers who were soldiers, he saw Goliath come out. Because David had a *different heart*, he didn't see Goliath as a giant but as a bully who was trying to take away the people's faith in God. David answered differently from all the thousands of soldiers who had been afraid. He said, 'Who is this Philistine that he should taunt the armies of the living God?' Then David took some stones and aimed at Goliath with his slingshot. He yelled, 'You come to me with a sword and a spear, but I come to you in the name of the Lord of hosts, the God of the army of Israel. Today the Lord will deliver you into my hands so that all the earth will know that there is one true God in Israel.'"

"Nate," I told my son, "all the other people, thousands and thousands of them, didn't even see God in their midst when the armies came into battle and the giant confronted them every day. They lived in fear because of what they could see with their *eyes*. But David saw with his *heart*. He saw this challenge as an opportunity to show the greatness of God. And David pleased God greatly because he didn't just say he loved God, but he showed it by his actions. That's the kind of love you so generously gave to me today, a love that considers how to give back and encourage."

And then I encouraged Nathan with a challenge similar to what my mother always said to me when she finished the story. "God showed that even a boy can do miracles if he believes in a great God. Even you might be used by God to do miracles, Nate, if you believe in our great God. You are a boy of action. Don't ever be afraid of giants in your life, and always remember to show your love and faith like you did today!"

Nate gave me another hug and kiss, then ran off to play.

I always loved telling this story to my children because it was the story that first stirred within my heart the desire to be a girl of action. Like every little girl, I wanted to do something great with my life, and this story and my mom's words added fuel to my soul's fire. The idea that God could use a normal person like me really captivated my interest. I wanted to be strong and brave like David. But even more than that, I admired that he was spunky, bold, and full of life. He had, as my mother repeated over and over, *a different heart.*

Let the heart of those who seek the LORD be glad.

1 CHRONICLES 16:10

A MAN WITH A DIFFERENT HEART

Whenever my mother told me the story of David, I would ask, "What does it mean to have a different heart?"

"Oh, that's the most important thing," she would say. "A person with a different heart doesn't see life as it appears on the outside. Instead, she sees life from the heart, the way God sees it. She follows what God tells her to do in her heart, not depending on what she sees with her eyes. So you need to learn how to see God with the eyes of your heart and follow what God shows you is really true. It's like looking for God's secrets as you would search for treasure. The ones who have different hearts find the treasures of heaven that God has strewn all throughout their lives so that they can always find joy wherever he is."

David had grasped the keys to a joyful life: to look at things through God's eyes, seeing *God's* reality and purposes; to search for the secrets of God as for treasure; to watch for God's shadow, his movement, his humor, his artistry everywhere, every day, and to respond to it. David didn't just see God's reality; he responded to it, just as Nathan had responded and reciprocated his love and praise to me!

As I began to diligently study the Bible on how to have a joyful life, I looked up the words *dancing* and *joy*. It was no surprise that my old hero, David, came up. In reading his stories again I remembered the words my mother impressed upon me about the life of this man and those important first steps to having the joyful life I was seeking: to look at life through the eyes of my heart, not just with my physical eyes.

Now, I realize this chapter has a lot of biblical references and background. But please bear with me because this sets the stage for so much that I want to share with you about how we can live in joy. David's story gave me a starting point, a biblical paradigm, for what it looks like to live a life of joy, recognizing and responding to the invisible yet strong presence of God daily, moment by moment. I am convinced that David's story shows us a life that can be danced and celebrated by everyday people like me and you.

With "heart" eyes, we learn to see God's power. We also learn to believe, as David did, that as the children of God the whole host of heaven is behind us. David approached Goliath in the name of the Lord of hosts! What a difference it would make if we lived as though the Lord of hosts and his army were with us every day, that he was protecting us, loving us, working his will for his good pleasure in the minutest details of our lives!

But as I studied further, I realized that David not only had a different heart but had a different attitude. It was revealed in his dance—the dance I saw him do in the other picture of him in my family Bible! Although the picture had puzzled me as a little girl, as an adult it became a paradigm of what joy should look like.

The picture showed David twirling around, wearing just a loincloth (it looked like underwear to me!), surrounded by a watching crowd. In the background stood a beautiful maiden with glossy dark hair, viewing David with scorn and embarrassment. I didn't blame her: David didn't look at all like a warrior in this picture; he looked like a silly man showing off.

But it was just this story that, years later, became for me a visible expression of biblical joy. As I viewed this story of David through the lens of "a man who had a different heart," that joy came alive for me. David danced before the Lord with all of his heart because he loved God; his dance poured out of the overflow of his relationship with God.

That seems easy enough to understand. But to truly appreciate the depth of his joy in that scene, we have to understand what had happened *before* David's dance.

Through Many Dangers, Toils, and Snares

Throughout their history, the Israelites continually rebelled against God and wanted to go their own way or mimic the way of others in the world.

When David was still a boy, God had desired to rule over the Jews personally. He had provided them with a name—Israel—a land, and the Law, to show them how to live. He gave them a means of knowing him and having his presence, protection, and blessing on their lives. His love and guidance would come through personal instruction in the Law, through his priests and prophets. He would be their leader and king.

But the Israelites wanted a human king, like the other nations. They wanted to have the status of a king, who would lead them into battle and have a palace and give them the self-imposed importance that the surrounding nations displayed.

God predicted that having a king would cost them greatly: taxes to pay for the king's house and servants; taking away their sons and daughters from their homes and moving them to the palace to serve this human king; requiring their lands and crops to benefit those at his own table. But still the people would not listen; they insisted on doing what seemed right in their own eyes (1 Samuel 8:11–18). So the nation was thrilled when, against God's wishes, he allowed them to turn from his leadership toward a hope that a man could save them and give them the status, security, and ease of life they longed to have.

Saul, their first king, was a man who looked the part. Scripture tells us that Saul was "a choice and handsome man, and there was not a more handsome person than he among the sons of Israel; from his shoulders and up he was taller than any of the people" (1 Samuel 9:2). Yet he proved unable to hold to God's standards. He took matters of Israel into his own hands repeatedly and in each situation brought devastation to his people. He based his decisions on what seemed right in his own eyes rather than pursuing God and serving him obediently.

Fast-forward a few years. God told Samuel, the prophet over Israel, that he had rejected Saul and wanted Samuel to anoint a new king, one who would obey and serve him. God's choice was David, a man of great contrast to Saul.

When Samuel went to anoint the next king, he first looked at David's older brother, Eliab, who appeared a worthy prospect. But God instructed him, "Do not look at his appearance or at the height of his stature, because I have rejected him; for God sees not as man sees, for man looks at the outward appearance, but the LORD looks at the heart" (1 Samuel 16:7).

This time the qualifications for leadership would not be based on a man's handsome or strong physical appearance but on the inner loyalties and habits of his heart; a devotion to God would qualify a man to be king. *David had a different heart*—his heart was focused on God.

As a shepherd boy, spending chilly nights under a rough blanket on the ground, gazing at the infinite stars twinkling in the open sky, David marveled at the handiwork of God. Hiking over the wildflower-covered, hot, sandy hills in summer to care for his noisy flock of sheep, and knowing well the constant care required of one watching over his flock, David wrote down his thoughts of a heavenly Shepherd who so directed his life. He sang to a God who led him to life-giving waters of refreshment and who became his constant companion.

Although David was anointed to become the next king of Israel, he would not take the throne for another twenty-five years, when he would finally dance. Those twenty-five years were filled with havoc, life-threatening danger, and rejection. Yet through these difficulties, David showed over and over his loyalty to and love for God.

David did not base his joy on his circumstances but on his perception of God's daily companionship. And his inner life and love for God grew stronger.

Then David spoke to the chiefs of the Levites to appoint their relatives the singers, with instruments of music, harps, lyres, loud-sounding cymbals, to raise sounds of joy.

1 CHRONICLES 15:16

GIVING LOVE JUST BECAUSE

One mysterious evening before we were married or even dating, I received a phone call from Clay. He asked if I was busy on the next Saturday, explaining that he wanted me to accompany him on a surprise adventure. "Sure!" I said.

Up to that point, we had been friends for a number of years but had both just recently moved to Denver and had been working in leadership together with a singles group in a local ministry.

I tried to get him to give me a hint of what the day would include, but all he would say was that it would take all day and that I needed to dress casually.

That Saturday he picked me up, and we drove on a winding road into the Rocky Mountains alongside the most beautiful clear stream. The countryside was covered with wildflowers—Indian paintbrush and blue gentians. The sky was bright blue, and a cool summer breeze wafted through the pungent air.

"According to my calculations, we're almost there," he declared.

Within minutes, he pulled up to a quaint Polish mountain chalet in the middle of nowhere. "This is it!" he said, smiling.

As we stepped through the wooden doorway, we were greeted by a hostess dressed in a traditional Polish costume. Thick woven wool tapestries covered the walls, intricately carved boxes and figurines decorated the shelves, and Polish chess sets were strewn around the room.

I couldn't believe it! It reminded me of my time as a missionary in Poland.

The hostess led us to a little wooden table with a vase full of wildflowers as its centerpiece.

"This is wonderful!" I told him as we ate a delicious Polish meal.

"I knew you would like this place since you were a missionary in Poland the last three years," he said. "I read about this restaurant in the newspaper and thought it would be a fun surprise for you."

We finished eating, and as we walked out the door, Clay turned to me with a twinkle in his eyes. "Just one more surprise left!"

As we drove back down the winding road toward home, he suddenly said, "This looks like just the place." He pulled off the road and parked next to a bubbling stream lined with an array of flowers. He pulled from the car trunk a blanket and a small cooler. Then he spread the blanket out next to the brook. He opened the cooler and took out luscious strawberries, Austrian chocolates, and some apple cider.

It was the perfect romantic setting.

"I wanted to make this day a special memory for you," Clay said. "I've really grown in my friendship with you over the years. I like who you are, I appreciate your convictions and your love for God, and I've developed a deep abiding love for you. So I wanted to give you a day filled with things that I knew would delight your heart.

"I used to make lists of the qualities I hoped to one day find in a wife," he continued. "But one day when I was reading my Bible, I realized that God's love for us isn't conditional because of what we've done to please him. He gives us his love freely because his *nature* is to love generously. So I decided that when I get married, God would want me to be committed to love a woman someday, not because she's perfect but because she's someone God has called me to love unconditionally and to give my life to, no matter what. So I threw away my list and asked God to show me how to develop that kind of generous love he has given to me. But I'm not coming to you because you meet all the expectations I once had on my list. I want you to know that out of all on the women I've met, I think I would love to be committed to give my love, as best I can, unconditionally to you, and to spend my life with you, giving to you as God has given to me."

I was so surprised by his words! All my life I felt that I had lived with conditional love. I had spent so much time and energy trying to do the right things in order to be loved. But here he was, saying that he wanted to be committed to loving me unconditionally in an act of faith and commitment; he wanted to model in our relationship the kind of love he had received and experienced from God. It was such a purehearted gift.

My heart overflowed with gratefulness and a natural responsive love. How could I not respond that way?

God wants that same natural outpouring from us. He has done so much to make our lives blessed, and he just wants us to *recognize* his great love. He wants us to respond to him out of an appreciative heart that treasures his gift of generous, thoughtful, and unconditional love—not because we have earned it or deserved it.

That was the kind of love that prompted David to break out in singing and dancing before his God.

THE DANCE WAS WORTH THE WAIT

Finally, a quarter of a century after his anointing, after a failed kingship in which the children of Israel were led away from God's ways, David took the throne. He had waited patiently through years of wandering, fighting battles, being falsely accused, and being rejected by Saul's loyal followers. These had been years of humbly trusting God for his perfect timing to crown him as king. Saul, who connived constantly to manipulate the details of his life in his favor, died in bitterness, defeat, and separation from God.

When David was able to move into Jerusalem to serve and rule over God's people, he planned a magnificent celebration, a splendid gala to bless and encourage all the families of Israel. It would be the fulfillment of God's prophecy. He ordered cakes baked and lambs roasted and provided a feast for thirty thousand (the leaders of Israel and all of their families). Seven bulls and seven rams were sacrificed in honor of God's presence (1 Chronicles 15:26). David arranged for the best musicians in the land to sing and to play in an orchestra to honor the coming of the ark of God back into their land.

He organized the Levites (the priests) to consecrate themselves before God (1 Chronicles 15:14); he arranged for the chiefs of the Levites to appoint for themselves a choir of singers and to bring an orchestra of musicians who would play harps, lyres, loud-sounding cymbals (verse 16). He even chose Chenaniah, chief of the Levites, to be in charge of singing because "he was skillful" (verse 22).

David and all the families of Israel would participate in the event, singing, dancing, celebrating, and shouting. He commanded them to "raise sounds of joy" (verse 16). It was a momentous festival to celebrate the return of the ark of God, which represented his presence among men, to Jerusalem. David recognized that the ark's presence was a tangible picture of man's deep need for God's abiding presence among them. That David wanted to bring the ark of God into Jerusalem was a sign of their leader's humble heart; he would reign only under the authority of God's presence and blessing. It was a sign of David's acknowledgment of God's rightful position in the lives of his people.

David wanted to be sure that everyone was clear about who the *real* king was: the Lord God whom he served.

David put on his best clothes (he was actually clothed in an ephod of fine linen, a beautiful garment worn by priests). And the elaborate, grand celebration began. The parade was elegant, organized, joyful, and fun. All the people of David's city were praising God, honoring and worshiping him as his presence came into their city. It was probably loud and boisterous. Imagine thirty thousand people dancing, shouting loudly, and playing instruments.

David became so overcome with joy because of what God had done for him that he began to leap and dance before the Lord. He danced—

and this is my picture of joy—with all his might for God and for God's glory! David jumping, wiggling, swirling, swinging with a heart filled with gladness. He was uninhibited in his celebration. A man of music, pulsing to the rhythms of horns and symbols, he was delighting with all of his heart in this party for his King. David was leading and modeling what pleased God—unabashed, humble, unpretentious celebration of the greatness of God.

David danced for joy before all of his people after persevering for many years. His dance was in the midst of the trials of middle-aged life, amongst the warp and woof of the dealings with his family, finances, wars, politics, and seasons.

David indeed had a *different heart*—his joy, his pleasure, his delight was in his God. The very words of one of his songs clearly declared this reality: "You will make known to me the path of life; in Your presence is fullness of joy; in Your right hand there are pleasures forever" (Psalm 16:11). Here was the heart's cry of this celebration: in God's presence was fullness of joy. David's response to this truth was not based on his circumstances, his battles, or his works but on knowing his God in and through the battles and victories of his life, and so dancing and celebration came as a result. He wasn't just *acting* joyful; loving God and seeing him with the eyes of his heart truly made David joyful.

And in this grand act of worship, he threw his whole being and heart into the magnificent expression of honoring God through unabashed dancing, "leaping and celebrating" (1 Chronicles 15:29). David was dancing before God—God, not man, was the recipient of his joyful and worshipful expression!

It was not an "act of obedience" dance; it was a "bubbling up from his heart" dance; not just words of love, but like Nathan, love turned to action and response.

Here was my picture of joy: David, having faithfully waited through years of anguish, danger, and humility, never lost his true focus on his ultimate Source of joy, his God, who had been with David every day, through every circumstance. And with his heart focused on the Source of his joy, David could leap and dance "before the LORD with all his might" (2 Samuel 6:14).

I believe that David saw in God great freedom—that his God created pleasure, color, beauty, food, love, sound, taste, and deep happiness. David was not tied up in knots of religion and rules, pretense and performance. Instead, he enjoyed and delighted in the God whom he knew to be his close friend and Lord. His dancing was a genuine expression of what he felt in his heart for his most beloved and intimate companion. Where had he learned this? Out in the fields, alone and free to ponder and live before God without pretense, being in nature with the stars and storms, seasons and changes. He'd been daily alone, living in the beauty of a world that displayed God's glory and handiwork. He'd spent many hours writing music about it, thinking about the Great Designer, and singing to an audience of one.

David's dance points the way to true, foundational, unchanging joy. His heart was indeed different. It was not focused on his circumstances or on the difficulties that had plagued his life, nor was his focus on pleasing others or fitting into their expectations. Instead he demonstrated single-minded concentration on the never-ending, living Source of joy—the Lord God himself. God, not distant, above in some remote heavenly place, but God real, present, involved in the earthy moments of life.

If the fruit of the Holy Spirit in our lives is joy, and if David illustrated in the Old Testament that in His presence is "fullness of joy," then that must be the answer to our search for a life of joy. In God, and him only, can we *find* joy, *understand* joy, *remain* in joy, and *celebrate* life each day with our hearts filled.

As I studied David's dance, his words in Psalm 100 came to mind:

Shout joyfully to the LORD, all the earth.

Serve the LORD with gladness;

Come before Him with joyful singing.

Know that the LORD Himself is God;

It is He who has made us, and not we ourselves;

We are His people and the sheep of His pasture. (verses 1–3)

It dawned on me anew that my response to God's reality in my life was not to be a duty or a work of obedience but an opportunity to see God for who he is—the Creator, Lover, Holy One, Shepherd, Savior, Friend, King. I think the reason God called David favored and what he so loved about this man was that David "got" him, that he never ceased to seek God and love him.

So where had my life veered from this pattern?

MY WRONG UNDERSTANDING OF GOD

I had been fostering a wrong understanding of God, mired in the details of life. I felt, at times, a subtle dread of him. Perhaps I was seeing the world around me with its sadness and difficulties as something God had caused, somehow not recognizing his presence with me in the midst of them. Subtle mental voices accused, *If God has allowed this, and it is a part of my life every day, then he must be somewhat of a kill-joy, a sort of spoiler of all that is fun and pleasurable.*

Whereas David celebrated God as the One who created laughter, beauty, pleasure, music, food, and goodness, Satan would love for me to believe that God is a spoiler—one who looks for my faults, who delights in making my life difficult and in ruining my hopeful expectation of what life *could* be. After all, didn't Satan start out by suggesting doubt in God's goodness to Adam and Eve? It seemed I had slowly forgotten that

God was good. I had inadvertently bought into Satan's suggestion that God was only interested in my dry obedience.

What if, in truth, our God is the party planner? (Didn't he say he was preparing a wedding feast for us and building mansions in heaven?) What if the same God who created a breathtaking garden, planned purpose and the love of family and friendship and the fulfillment of productive work, who delighted in children, who touched the sick and rejected, and who gave grace to the prostitutes and tax collectors *is* the God whose companionship we can enjoy each day?

As I thought on this, I realized that duty, forced obedience, and works never satisfied my soul or fooled my mind into thinking that dry acquiescence to spiritual dogma was equivalent to being a Christian who really knew and loved God. Knowing God deeply, intimately, personally within the borders of my own personality was what I hungered and thirsted for. I wanted to dance as David danced!

When a maiden is in love with her dance partner, she is delighted in the dance, totally engaging her heart with her beloved partner. She looks into his eyes, seeing his admirable qualities, living in the deep joy of the moment of being held in her lover's arms.

My dance, however, had become a hollow performance. I was in danger of becoming like the church in Ephesus, whom Jesus confronted in Revelation 2. At first he commended them: "I know your deeds and your toil and perseverance, and that you cannot tolerate evil men, and you put to the test those who call themselves apostles, and they are not, and you found them to be false; and you have perseverance and have endured for My name's sake, and have not grown weary" (verses 2–3).

What a great list of accomplishments for any mature believer! It even reflected so much of my life—choosing to believe in God, holding up his ideals, standing for truth and biblical theology, putting one foot in front of the other, and enduring great trials through so many seasons.

But then Jesus said, "But I have this against you, that you have left your first love. Therefore remember from where you have fallen, and repent and do the deeds you did at first" (verses 4–5).

So it wasn't just me who wanted to regain my old joy—the joy of my salvation! It was God himself who wanted this too. He missed the "me" of the old days, when I so freely loved him, believed in miracles, and was filled with hope and joy. He instructed me to "remember from where you have fallen."

I thought, *Remember—from where have I fallen?* When I first fell in love with the Lord, I was so much happier. I was willing to read my Bible for hours, hungering for understanding and truth, discussing into the wee hours of night with my college friends the wonderful truths I had never heard before. Praying fervently and eagerly awaiting miracles was the call of my heart. Enthusiastically I would foray into the lives of strangers, eager to tell them about his redemption and grace. Seeing a full harvest moon wafting across the sky would bring praise and appreciation to my lips. Fellowship with other believers was sweet and intimate. My whole life was genuinely wrapped up in God, not in a religious ritual but in an excited, passionate, grateful, purposeful way.

That was the place I had left, the place from where I had fallen. Since then, mundane duty had propelled me forward through the many corridors of my life. Yes, I'd enjoyed occasional waves of excitement and a heart choosing to love him. It is the commitment of my heart. But more often I'd been just putting one foot in front of the other. I wished for the reality of God to be true, but sometimes I had difficulty believing it or grasping him. I was living in obedience and cultivating faithful character, but often I would feel no emotion. I would drag through some of the days and give the party lines that people had come to expect from me, but I definitely was not dancing and celebrating. Now I realized I wanted so much more than a spiritual theology or a philosophy; I wanted a real, living, intimate relationship with the One I originally had learned to cherish the most.

Somehow, I knew instinctively that this deep desire to love God with abandon was a remnant of his touch on my life, a shadow of his reality, a part of the intrinsic design for which I had been made. My Creator had prewired me with the ability to celebrate life and to drink deeply from the well of emotions and pleasure wrought by his own hand.

When entering the corridors of heaven, finally meeting Jesus face to face, I do not want to arrive gasping, out of breath, desperate, barely making it over the finish line. Instead I want to enter resiliently with a hopeful, loving heart. If joy, satisfaction, and fulfillment are what God desires for me, then God created me with those capacities so that he could fill them. God disdains dry, mundane obedience as much as I do! He wants true, pure-of-heart, devoted love—to be shared in a personal, vibrant relationship. The very One who created the wild, lively winds, the intense beauty of storms, waterfalls, sunsets, and music of nature is the One who wants me to love and enjoy him amidst the dance of my life.

And those who were seen dancing were thought
to be insane by those who could not hear the music.

Friedrich Wilhelm Nietzsche

What Refusing to Dance Produces

I discovered one final thing about David's dance.

When David was leading all the people in a procession and praising God, his wife, Michal, evidently stayed home. What was she doing at home when thirty thousand Israelites were celebrating the coming of

God's presence through the ark? Well, she was Saul's daughter, a child of a king of Israel. She likely had been raised to think herself above the "common people," the very people whose sacrifice had made her rich life possible. Her heart must have been affected by the false supposition that she was superior.

Safely tucked away from the rabble, during the peak of the celebration, she looked out her window and saw her husband, the humble shepherd king, worshiping God and dancing with all the people. Scripture says that when she saw David doing this, "she despised him in her heart" (2 Samuel 6:16). That which was pleasing to God—the acknowledgment of his place among the Israelites, David's wholehearted worship of God, and as a king, leading them to worship God—was despicable to her.

So Michal criticized David for dancing in front of all the people and communicated her disdain toward him. Perhaps she had loved the glory, the pretense of her father's kingdom, and resented David mixing with the common people. Scripture doesn't tell us what led her to this point. What is clear is that David pleased God and Michal did not. She could not hear the music of God. She thought David insane. Yet even in this, we see a humble response from David. "It was before the LORD, who chose me above your father and above all his house, to appoint me ruler over the people of the LORD, over Israel; therefore I will celebrate before the LORD." God was his audience, not people. He was "humble in [his] own eyes" (2 Samuel 6:21–22).

The interesting result of Michal's response to David was that she was barren the rest of her life, one of the most embarrassing and cursed states for women in all of Israel. Perhaps the Lord was making a statement: barrenness of the soul will be the consequence of refusing to praise, worship, celebrate, and delight in the Lord's true character and declining to dwell in the presence of God.

Clearly joy is an issue of the heart. Joy is not found in performing for people or in doing all the right things for God. Nor is joy in the absence of difficulties or problems.

Joy is found in the presence of God in the midst of all circumstances, in delighting in the life he has given.

As David had a different heart, one that saw God every day, that praised and worshiped God without the pretense of religion but from the heart in sincerity and humility, so I needed my heart to be. I wanted to be like David, to get rid of pretense and performance. But to do that, I had to look at my heart and ask, *Have I become bitter, railing sometimes against what has happened in my life, and shut God out? Is my heart more like that of David: humble, thankful, worshipful? Or perhaps more like that of Michal, who had fostered pride and resentment in her heart?*

If David was right to declare of God "in Your presence is fullness of joy" and "in Your right hand there are pleasures forever" (Psalm 16:11), then that was where I needed to find it—in his presence. So my search for joy started with learning to experience God's presence, to see the facets of his reality every day.

Finding *Your* Rhythm in God's Joy

1. Psalm 16:11 says, "You will make known to me the path of life; in Your presence is fullness of joy; in Your right hand there are pleasures forever." David found strength and great joy in knowing God in the midst of his difficulties. He was not a perfect man; he made mistakes just like you and I do. But that didn't affect his confidence in his relationship with his God.

Write down the adjectives that describe what you find in your heart's relationship with God (fear, disillusionment, condemnation, contentment, doubt, happiness).

What specific obstacles keep you from experiencing God's love and joy?

Where does this passage tell us we will find joy? What does that mean to you?

2. James 4:4 says, "You adulteresses, do you not know that friendship with the world is hostility toward God? Therefore whoever wishes to be a friend of the world makes himself an enemy of God."

What does this passage say are the consequences of
being a friend with the world?

3. Saul had ruled by his own thoughts, will, and prowess and led
    the people into spiritual devastation. David wanted to conse-
    crate his kingship on the understanding that he was merely a
    servant of God and that only when God was exalted in their
    midst would Israel be blessed. You might say that Saul was a
    picture of following the world and David was a picture of fol-
    lowing God. These men reflected two different kinds of heart
    allegiance: one leading the people to vanity, one leading the
    people to God and to life.

    What style of living do you see more of yourself in,
    Saul's or David's?

    What could you change to bring your life more in
    line with how David lived his life?

In what ways are you seeking other people's approval?
How do you need to change?

4. Read Psalm 100:1–3: "Shout joyfully to the LORD, all the
   earth. Serve the LORD with gladness; come before Him with
   joyful singing. Know that the LORD Himself is God; it is He
   who has made us, and not we ourselves; we are His people
   and the sheep of His pasture."

What attitude is reflected in this verse that tells us our
rightful position with God?

What does it mean for your life that we are the sheep
of his pasture?

Are you willing to let God lead and be the Shepherd, or are you running away and hiding from your Shepherd?

5. In Revelation 2:4–5, Jesus said, "But I have this against you, that you have left your first love. Therefore remember from where you have fallen, and repent and do the deeds you did at first."

Ask yourself if you have fallen. Is your heart loving God generously? How could you get back to your first love of Christ?

6. Recognize that nothing apart from the Source of true joy can bring joy. Commit to put aside anything else you are depending on for your joy.

Dear heavenly Father,

I long to live freely in your joy. I want to love you with all my heart, for all the days of my life. Please meet me at my point of need. Show me your reality and heal my heart of any wrong ideas about you. Take away the burden of striving, so that I may enjoy each day, really knowing the reality of your presence. I love you, Lord. Amen.

Letting Go to Take
God's Hand

Last spring at a conference where I was speaking, a young woman stepped up to me and, with a very formal air, put out her hand to shake mine.

"Mrs. Clarkson," she said, "I know you are busy, but I was wondering if I could buy you a cup of tea and talk to you for a few minutes?"

The urgency in her voice and pleading of her eyes convinced me that I needed to meet with her. As I followed her to the hotel café, I noticed she was dressed in an obviously expensive black silk business suit and strode along confidently in high-heeled black pumps. I sensed she was a career woman who preferred life to be impeccable, sophisticated, and posh. Her makeup was perfect. Her hair was cut in sharp angles—very contemporary.

To be honest, I felt a little intimidated. Maybe she just threatened me because she looked so perfect, and I am not exactly the "perfect" type. Yet I was struck by more than just her fashion style. She exuded an almost palpable ice-cold, calculated demeanor that erected a barrier against anyone who would intrude into her inner world. I wondered what lay beneath this woman's exterior.

She headed toward a dark, secluded corner booth in the back of the café. We both eased into the shadowy seats. After ordering for both of us, she began matter-of-factly. "I'll get to the point. I'm a little embarrassed to tell you my story. I don't like to admit failure. But I feel that I need to talk to someone."

I nodded, encouraging her to continue and intrigued to learn what could possibly be so urgent and terrible.

"My family was poor, and we moved a lot," she began. "At a young age I determined that when I became an adult I would never allow myself to experience the humiliation or the insecurity I had felt as a young child. I loved my parents, and they were devoted to me, their only child, but all I dreamed of for years was getting away from home and making myself better. I intended to secure the best education and the best and highest paying job. And I was determined that if I ever had children, they would have the best that money could buy—a nice house, opportunities, new clothes. No hand-me-downs from cousins. They would never feel deprived as I had been in my childhood.

"After college, I became a Christian. I focused on learning as much of the Bible as I could. I gave my tithe, taught Bible studies for young women, and went to church every week. I like doing things the right way, and that's what I tried to do in my faith. But it never really seemed to fulfill me."

She paused for a sip of her tea, then continued.

"Professionally, I climbed the corporate ladder by working long hours and making myself as useful as possible to my bosses, so that they would always consider me for a better position. This success in my job gave me freedom to buy a beautiful home and the car I wanted. I still found myself feeling a hollow emptiness inside, even though I had been putting my best effort into making my life successful.

"During that time I met my husband. He's very handsome, which is what attracted me to him. We got married, and almost immediately I became pregnant. I thought that finally my life would be complete. I would have everything."

I could almost picture her with a checklist in hand, marking off each new accomplishment and asset.

"When my daughter was born, she was pronounced as a 'failure to thrive' baby. For the next ten months, she was in and out of hospitals. I really struggled with what was happening and thought, *Why can't I have a normal, pretty child like everyone else?* She's okay now, and I do love her, but I've had to give up a lot of my time to take care of her. I resent that sometimes.

"I became so anxious that I developed a nervous disorder. And after visiting numerous doctors, they put me on medication. Over the next two years, to help me deal with my nerves, my husband and I overspent on vacations that made me happy for a while. But the trips put us into thousands of dollars of debt. We had to move out of my nice house into a very middle-class neighborhood, which is so embarrassing that I won't invite people over—not even from church. Our house just doesn't reflect what I feel I'm really like."

She took another sip of her tea. I waited for her to continue, sensing there was still more to her story.

"My husband bores me. He's nice enough, but he just doesn't seem exciting anymore. I know I'm not supposed to get a divorce, but the thought of living with him seems so empty without more romance. I thought maybe another child would cheer me up, but I'm afraid to get pregnant again until I can move into a better house. I'm so unhappy. I feel so disillusioned. Nothing in my life has fulfilled me like I thought it would. I've tried so hard, and all I get for my effort is another problem. And God doesn't seem to hear my prayers about any of it. Every time I pray, he doesn't answer. Instead of the blessings I thought I'd have, I've just been cursed. I feel very cynical about my faith and bitter about how badly my life turned out. What should I do?"

> We are half-hearted creatures, fooling about with drink
> and sex and ambition when infinite joy is offered us, like
> an ignorant child who wants to go on making mud pies in
> a slum because he cannot imagine what is meant by the
> offer of a holiday at the sea. We are far too easily pleased.
>
> C. S. LEWIS

I WILL BE HAPPY WHEN...

As I listened to this "perfect" woman go on about how miserable she was and how much God had let her down, I found myself feeling very much as if I were sitting with a toddler who was having a tantrum. I hardly knew where to begin with her. So before I tried to answer her question, I prayed silently, *Lord, help me make her understand that now that she has come to the end of her own strength and spent the last of her personal resources trying to provide for herself, she is in a great place to start the journey toward real joy, which can come only by allowing you to guide her in* your *ways.*

In the midst of my prayer, this young woman became a mirror to me. I realized that I had been in her shoes at one time in my life, even though my circumstances had been different.

After I became a committed Christian in college, I worked my way to righteousness: I attended church and Bible studies, tithed, and finally decided to go into Christian work. And I sort of expected, though perhaps subconsciously, that God would bless my obedience by giving me everything I desired in life: marriage, family, success in my work.

My first thought had been, *I will be happy when I get married.* I finally got married at twenty-eight. Since I equated happiness with achieving my ideals in my life, I was surprised when my marriage didn't soothe the restlessness in my spirit and fill the vacuum in my heart.

I thought a child might fulfill me. So I prayed, *Lord, please bless me with a child.* I became pregnant at thirty-one. I gave birth to three babies in the next five years, which left me reeling! Instead of feeling fulfilled, I found myself overwhelmed with the responsibility of motherhood.

I was blessed with three children and married to my best friend. But my best friend worked seventy hours a week, leaving me to handle the house and parenting responsibilities mostly on my own. I felt alone. I had few friends because we moved every two years into new ministry situations.

I kept finding myself thinking, *I will be happy when…* And I filled in the blanks with a list of events I had built up in my mind, which I was certain would fulfill my life.

I will be happy when all of my babies are out of diapers.

I will be happy when we have friends and support systems.

I will be happy when my husband is home more.

I will be happy when we can change jobs.

I will be happy when we have a bigger salary.

The list marched subconsciously through my mind each day of my discontent. And with each passing day, my dissatisfaction and expectations grew. During this time, I was reading my Bible and serving God the best I knew how. I didn't realize that I mistakenly believed I needed these things to be happy because I was basing my expectations on worldly, temporal values.

Finally, I came to the end of myself. At some point in life, it dawned on me that this is the "broken place." Earth is the temporary place where Satan rules and where all people are sinful and subject to the disappointments of a fallen world, to the longings that come from being separated from God. I can picture ideals and dream of the life for which I was created, but Jesus never promised I would experience ultimate fulfillment in this world.

I realized that if I didn't build my foundations on eternal realities, I would never be content. Nothing in this physical world would ever totally live up to my expectations. The Lord had to dissolve my self-will in a slow, humbling process of my reluctantly giving up my ideas about what I needed to be happy. I had to become willing to place myself on the altar of God's will. Trying to control my life and whip it into shape by means of my own effort only brought frustration and disillusionment. I realized that in a fallen world, happiness, perfection, and the fairy tale of a Cinderella life are always doomed to failure.

I had to relinquish all the treasures—my expectations about life and God and relationships—that I held tightly in my fist. But it didn't happen overnight. It was a slow process. It took me a long time to realize that I had spent years telling God what my life should be and how I expected him to follow my plans.

Now don't get me wrong. I enjoyed many wonderful pleasures and close relationships along the way. But part of my problem was that I wasn't prepared for what real life would hold. I was surprised by many of the normal issues of life and how burdensome they were—the huge amounts of work that it takes to make a home, the demanding task of caring for children, the give and take required in a marriage, the bills that arrive every month and still have to be paid! I was immature and didn't even *know* that I lacked character!

The most amazing realization was that God didn't force my false treasures from my hands. He gently took them one at a time. And with each relinquishment I discovered I could trust him. With each I found that I had a peace and freedom from performance that I had never experienced. I began to feel less pressure and burden to succeed in life and more satisfaction and childlike enjoyment in my days. When my hands were empty of vain expectations, I was able to hold God's hand and began to learn my first few dance steps.

EXPECTATIONS VERSUS REALITY!

The Holy Spirit was reminding me of these things and of my journey as I sat across the café table from this anxious woman, who was so obviously unhappy and hurting. She had spent her whole life building unrealistic dreams, only to have them blown away in the misty, mysterious winds of life. I knew her situation was not a lost cause. But to make the needed changes, she would first need to uncover those things—the real issues of her heart—that had kept her from true fulfillment and heartfelt joy. No thing, person, or experience had ever satisfied her. What was missing that she had been trying to find every place she had journeyed? She also needed to closely examine her view of God and the Christian life. Her expectations were that if she just found the right formula, followed it, and worked it enough, she would find the success, intimacy, and ultimate happiness that had been eluding her.

As we spoke, it became obvious that self-absorption and self-centeredness were clouding her mind against all reason—even to the point where she didn't seem to feel any authentic concern for her husband, child, parents, or anyone else. It was all about her. She was unable to grasp what God really wanted to do in her life and what that would mean for her.

"Ultimately, I feel so depressed," she pronounced at the end of our meeting. "I don't see any way forward that will meet my needs."

This woman had ordered the external areas of her life, supposing that the right arrangement would bring joy and peace. Yet joy is a fruit of the Holy Spirit; it comes not from outside circumstances but from within ourselves as we learn to appreciate the values of God's kingdom. Grasping and working diligently to provide for her own needs, she was looking for joy in all the wrong places. She had become exhausted in working so hard to do the things that would never satisfy. Oh, how I wished I could transfer to her some of my own hard-earned insights!

When I was newly married, my husband, Clay, had to work long hours at seminary in order to finish school quickly. One day I planned a surprise for him. I cooked his favorite meal of parmesan chicken, set our little table with the sparkling new china and silver we had received as wedding presents, lit candles, put on soft music, and then I put on a special dress. I had a lot of time on my hands because I had no job since we had moved to a new town for Clay to attend seminary. So all day as I waited for him to get home from his heaviest day of classes, I built up all sorts of expectations about how romantic an evening we would have together.

Meanwhile, he had been working, studying, and attending classes all day. When he arrived home, he was exhausted.

"Oh, I ate a sandwich between two classes," he said casually. "Thanks for cooking. It looks great, but I'm not hungry. I have to go study for a final tomorrow. You enjoy yourself." And off he went to work on a paper.

I was boiling mad. I was doing something to "serve" him, but in reality I expected him to tell me what a wonderful wife I was, and what a good cook I was, and how beautiful I was, and how fortunate he was to be married to me! He never knew what hit him when I exploded all over him.

These kinds of expectations are typical in marriage. But such unrealistic expectations set us up for failure because we aim for fulfillment in the wrong places.

I often meet with women who are distraught, upset, and feel distant from God. Though usually very sincere of heart and wanting to walk with God, they find great disappointment and disillusionment because they have believed in the religious formulas they've been taught. They don't realize that their prayers and lives have been more about building up the kinds of expectations that I had with Clay, about what they hoped life would be and then telling God how he should act on their behalf: "God, since I'm a reasonably mature adult and I think I know what would be the optimum way for you to work in my life, I want you to bless my plan. Please give me healthy kids, when I want them—I'll use birth control until I'm ready, and then I want you to work a miracle. And I'd like a good marriage, a nice salary, a lovely home. Help me not to be lonely or think disquieting thoughts or... I know you will come through for me because I'm coming to you in faith and in the name of Jesus."

And then these unintentionally misguided women go their own way, building their lives on foundations that are not biblical and not cultivating a heart for what Scripture tells us is God's way. The result is, then, that they haven't really had fellowship with God at all, and they wonder where he has gone—when their lives are a result of their own actions and self-centered choices.

My Journey Toward an Unpredictable God

As I look back over the years, I can see the point at which the Lord began to work a new paradigm into my life. As I started working with a Christian student organization upon graduating from college, one of my directors encouraged me to spend a day alone with the Lord to plan my year of ministry. I was so young and inexperienced and green, but of course I didn't know I was! I thought my passionate heart would make up for my lack of experience and wisdom.

I reserved a room at a local hotel and intended to spend a day praying and planning my year. Beginning with a solemn and serious heart, I prayed about everything I could think of and felt I was being quite spiritual. When I looked at my watch, however, only twenty minutes had passed! What in the world was I going to do with the rest of my day? So I prayed a few minutes more and then started to flip through my Bible.

I came to a passage in Philippians 3:7–9. Paul was explaining the process of maturity and commitment that he made when he had committed his life to Christ:

> But whatever things were gain to me, those things I have counted as loss for the sake of Christ. More than that, *I count all things to be loss in view of the surpassing value of knowing Christ Jesus my Lord, for whom I have suffered the loss of all things, and count them but rubbish so that I may gain Christ*, and may be found in Him, not having a righteousness of my own derived from the Law, but that which is through faith in Christ, the righteousness which comes from God on the basis of faith.

My heart was drawn to this verse in which Paul expressed what I wanted: to *really* know God, to understand the truth about life, to be purposeful, and to invest in a meaningful life. Paul seemed to be saying, "Everything else is worthless to me in comparison to the great treasure of being able to know God completely and deeply."

As I sat in that hotel room, I clung to that verse. My faith meant more to me than anything else. I prayed, *God, I want to make this commitment to you: that the most important thing to me in the world is to know you and love you! So though I have never lost much in my life and I don't truly know what it means to give up everything, I want to have a heart that would be willing to do that. I commit my life anew into your hands and ask you to show me what this means.*

All these years later, I look back and see that I was like a little girl who dresses up in her mother's high-heeled shoes and ball gown and pretends to be a real princess. I was attempting to put on the attitude and demeanor of the great saint, Paul. Yet I no more understood what it meant to give up all things in my life, to count them but rubbish in order to gain Christ, than a child knows what it means to be royalty. I wasn't even aware that I had a hold on so many things—or should I say, I didn't know so many things had a hold on me!

I was convinced that everything I wanted was essential to my happiness; those things that I thought I needed or deserved in order to be happy and fulfilled, joyful and complete: the family, the right missionary placement, the best job, the right house. I was grasping at everything the world had to offer to give me ultimate joy. Not realizing it, I had built values in my heart and a foundation for a kingdom that was pretty much dependent on this world and on people rather than on God.

I thought marriage and romance would make me feel loved and lovable; a career as a professional speaker and writer would give me worth and value; as a mother, my children would fulfill the longing to be cherished and revered; friends and family would gratify my need to be liked and appreciated; a beautiful house and yard and material trappings of the world would keep me satisfied. I was reaching for all the things I thought would bring me joy instead of reaching for the *true* source of joy—God Himself. Psalm 16:11 says, "In Your presence is fullness of joy; in Your right hand there are pleasures forever." I needed to reach for the One who created joy in order that I might be truly fulfilled and at peace.

Yet even in my young, naive state, from that moment in the hotel room, I believe that God very gently took me at my word. He knew that I was clinging to so many things tightly, not recognizing them as rubbish, and he patiently opened my eyes and heart to the truth.

The journey to find the genuine treasure of knowing God has led over a rough and difficult road of relinquishing my "rights" and clinging to God's desires. My hands have gripped hard at times, when I wasn't sure if I could truly trust that God was in control and wanted the best for me. At times, I would throw tantrums when I didn't feel that God heard and answered my demands for fulfillment.

What I have found, though, is that God is not threatened or moved by my tantrums. He knows what I really need, and he, like any good parent, is willing to bear with my accusations of him, knowing that ultimately his way will bring freedom and deep, satisfying joy. He knows that if my heart is tuned to him and if I love him, after whining against his discipline and after resisting him, he will yield in my life the results of a mature character and divine fruit.

It simply takes opening my hands to hold God's hand so he can train and grow me.

All discipline for the moment seems not to be joyful,
but sorrowful; yet to those who have been trained by it,
afterwards it yields the peaceful fruit of righteousness.

HEBREWS 12:11

A FATHER'S TRAINING

In Hebrews 12:9–10, the author compares God's training and discipline of his children to that of a real father who disciplines his son. "We had earthly fathers to discipline us, and we respected them; shall we not much rather be subject to the Father of spirits [our spiritual Father], and live? For they [our fathers] disciplined us for a short time as seemed best to them, but He [God] disciplines us for our good, so that we may share His holiness."

Many of us think of this passage only in terms of the discipline God brings. But it's also a passage that leads up to joy. God's discipline and training is for our good. Not for God's good as though he is a capricious dictator, but for *our* good! His ultimate goal, though, is truly wonderful: that we might share in his holiness. God wants us to have his perfect character—the attributes of God that we observed in Christ. Just as a father who loves his child disciplines him that he might become excellent, so God disciplines us that we might have the excellencies of Christ.

The next verse deals specifically with the joy that we seek: "All discipline for the moment seems *not to be joyful, but sorrowful.*" So a part of the journey toward joy is sorrow. How true! My journey toward God and toward joy has truly been filled with sorrow and sadness. Disappointment in so many things—people, experiences, possessions, churches, Christians, even life itself! But the rest of the verse indicates that eventually joy will come: "Yet to those who have been trained by it [discipline], afterwards it yields the peaceful fruit of righteousness."

The process of changing my whole life paradigm from holding on to what I thought would bring me joy to learning God's way led me through many valleys of despair and depression. But it's brought me to the fruit of righteousness, to joy.

Too often we think that God should just pour out joy without growing us into it. Patience, long-suffering, and self-discipline are not exactly popular in our culture. Instant gratification at whatever the cost is generally the way of our world.

It's taken me years to understand the nature of training and that from training comes a more mature character and the joy that I seek. The length of time that training requires has taught me the value of endurance. Gold medal Olympians undergo many, many years of training before they become the best in the world. Many good athletes give up before reaching their goal, unwilling to face the grueling days of arduous exercise, losses, successes, failures. Only the one who hangs in there, who keeps going even through the difficult seasons, will have the glory of winning the medal. Finally, the athlete achieves his goal—and he also has gained strength, skill, and excellence in his character.

Spiritual training, too, takes place over a long period of time—from baby to mature adult; from immaturity to godly wisdom. Learning to dance isn't an instant accomplishment; it's a lengthy process of learning (and sometimes relearning) to let go of these things that bind us in order to be free to hold the hand of the Lord, as he is the source of joy. He will teach us the dance, but we first must empty our hands so that we are free to hold his hand.

Sadly, the woman in the café, for all her troubles, was unable to let go of those things that brought her discontent. And because of it she dealt with anxiety, depression, and disillusionment.

Truth and Consequences

Many years ago, I attended a counseling seminar that helped me understand depression more clearly. The instructor explained that most often, depression comes from disappointed expectation. The expectation doesn't even have to be realistic or valid. It can be an expectation that marriage or motherhood is an instant road to happiness or fulfillment or feeling loved or having someone meet your needs. It can be tied to having certain material things, like an expensive car, a nice home, a higher paying job—or to specific experiences, such as taking a family trip to Disneyland or moving to a different place. It can be connected to an unsatisfied desire for a better family or background or—you can fill in the blank. But when the expectations go unmet—or the long-anticipated event arrives without bringing happiness—depression and anger are the natural consequences.

Many people spend their whole lives trying to shape circumstances, people, and things to fit their expectations; they take life into their own hands and strive to attain those things, experiences, and relationships that they believe will fulfill their deepest longings. Materialism, experiences, beauty, and success define much of our current culture; we're led to believe we can find happiness through owning the right things, establishing a relationship with the perfect sex partner, attaining the right status, earning the right college degree, or achieving the right weight and having the perfect body.

Yet Scripture is clear that none of these things will truly satisfy. Jesus said that he who builds his life on such false foundations will experience a great fall. He admonished, "Do not store up for yourselves treasures on earth, where moth and rust destroy, and where thieves break in and steal. But store up for yourselves treasures in heaven, where neither moth nor rust destroys, and where thieves do not break in or steal; for where your treasure is, there your heart will be also" (Matthew 6:19–21).

Our heart will not, *cannot,* be with God if it is focused on seeking happiness apart from him.

Later, in chapter 7:26–27, at the culmination of this sermon, Jesus warned about building the foundations of one's life on things that cannot satisfy: "Everyone who hears these words of Mine and *does not* act on them, will be like a foolish man who built his house on the sand. The rain fell, and the floods came, and the winds blew and slammed against that house; and it fell—and great was its fall."

This whole story indicates that rain will come and the winds will burst against us in this life. We were made for gladness of heart and joy, but in this world, which is wildly rebellious to God and his ways, storms will indeed come and rage against our souls. What determines whether such storms will destroy our happiness or push us toward it is whether we struggle against the wind or let it push us toward God.

Recently, as I was reading the book *Rilla of Ingleside* to my youngest daughter, I realized the story puts its finger on what we can potentially gain from the sadness and difficulty that so often come into our lives.

Rilla, the protagonist, is the youngest child of the famed Anne of Green Gables—the sixth book in the series of Anne's story. The story begins in 1914 when Rilla is fifteen. She is a carefree, fun, dreamy-eyed teenager who has great hopes for a romantic life. The book opens with Rilla's first dance, which she hopes will be an evening of intrigue and romance. It starts out so, and yet quickly is spoiled by the excited announcement that a great war has started in Europe, which becomes the beginning of World War I.

As the story develops over the next two years, Rilla's whole life must change because of the difficulties and demands the war places on her and her family. Food rationing depletes the storehouse of their tasty food. She becomes the primary caretaker of an abandoned war baby, which totally changes her carefree lifestyle. Her brothers and childhood chums all leave to become soldiers in the trenches of France and Italy, so she is forced to confront loneliness. Her life becomes consumed with worry and waiting as she works with the Red Cross to help take care of returning soldiers.

Throughout those two years, an immature, young, self-centered girl blossoms beautifully into a young woman, strong, patient, capable, and life-giving to those around her. A friend reflects with her over the changes.

> "Two years ago this morning I woke wondering what delightful gift the new day would give me. These are the two years I thought would be filled with fun."
>
> "Would you exchange them—now—for two years filled with fun?"
>
> "No," said Rilla slowly, "I wouldn't. It's strange—isn't it?— They have been two terrible years—and yet I have a queer feeling of thankfulness for them—as if they had brought me something

very precious, with all their pain. I wouldn't *want* to go back and be the girl I was two years ago, not even if I could. Not that I think I've made any wonderful progress—but I'm *not* quite the selfish, frivolous little doll I was then. I suppose I had a soul then, Miss Oliver—but I didn't know it. I know it now—and that is worth a great deal—worth all the suffering of the past two years. And still…I don't *want* to suffer any more—not even for the sake of more soul growth. At the end of two more years I might look back and be thankful for the development they had brought me, too; but I don't want it now."

"We never do," said Miss Oliver. "That is why we are not left to choose our own means and measure of development, I suppose. No matter how much we value what our lessons have brought us we don't want to go on with the bitter schooling."[1]

How true these comments ring for me. Even though I want to be holy and I know that disappointment eventually yields the fruit of joy, I still don't look forward to discipline or sadness. But that does not mean I am unspiritual. We were all made to have joy, to be glad, and to delight in life. Yet we also were made to be like Jesus, to have his character. And so God disciplines us and allows us to endure disappointment for our good, that we may be greatly blessed with a deeper heart that is able to appreciate the real treasure of life.

THE BACKWARD WAY TO JOY

As I have been studying this biblical concept of joy, at times I have wanted to rename this book *The Backwards Book*. So many of the things we think will bring us joy instead bring only emptiness. And the way to joy is through a pathway of sorrow, which we naturally resist.

Perhaps this is what Jesus meant when he said, "If anyone wishes to come after Me, he must deny himself, and take up his cross daily and follow Me. For whoever wishes to save his life will lose it, but whoever loses his life for My sake, he is the one who will save it. For what is a man profited if he gains the whole world, and loses or forfeits himself?" (Luke 9:23–25).

Yes, God's desire is for us to experience true joy and deep fulfillment. It must start, however, with the journey into the recesses of our heart. It is only as we release our hold on the things that we *think* we need to be truly happy, when we open our hands freely, that we experience true joy. We yield our demands and expectations to him so that we may take his hand and let him lead us into the dance of joy. He is the One who will teach us. But it requires a total relinquishment of self and a simple trust in a great God, simple faith to understand that he who created joy will lead us on the pathway that ends in the joy that will last forever.

Are you willing to give away all that you think is valuable in order to find all that truly has worth?

Finding *Your* Rhythm in God's Joy

1. Matthew 6:19–21 says, "Do not store up for yourselves treasures on earth, where moth and rust destroy, and where thieves break in and steal. But store up for yourselves treasure in heaven, where neither moth nor rust destroys, and where thieves do not break in and steal; for where your treasure is, there your heart will be also."

What are the treasures on earth that you have looked to for happiness or fulfillment?

What do you think the treasures of heaven are? How do you look for these treasures?

2. In Matthew 6:33, Jesus said, "Seek first His kingdom and His righteousness, and all these things will be added to you."

What does it mean, practically and in your heart, to seek first the kingdom of God?

Name five ways that God wants you to do this.

3. According to Hebrews 12:10, God disciplines us "that we may share His holiness." In what areas has he disciplined you? In what ways are you being disciplined now?

What does God promise will be the result of submitting to his discipline? (Look at Hebrews 12:11 if you need a hint.)

Dear heavenly Father,

I thank you that you have my best in mind when you direct my life in difficult places. Open the eyes of my heart that I may see your love in the midst of my own suffering. Help me to see clearly the blessings that you have brought from these lessons in the past. I want to relinquish all of the earthly things I have been depending on for my joy, and I ask you to fill me with the joy that comes from holding your hand and knowing you are with me every step of my life. In Jesus' name I come to you. Amen.

Four

Dancing Through the Twists and Turns of Life

In moving through life's pathway, we often miss the heavenly applause and the angelic fanfare that mark our seemingly ordinary moments. Focused on our outward performance, we overlook the spiritual reality of inner victories and heart growth as we face each day with courage. Yet our invisible God sees such moments as the significant occasions of our lives, where greatness is forged through secret choices of faith seen only by him. I learned this lesson through my sweet then-thirteen-year-old daughter, Joy, who demonstrated her growing faith in the midst of trying circumstances.

Last fall, after garnering airline points for several years, my two daughters, a friend of mine, and I decided to take a trip together to England to visit the homes of some of our favorite classic English authors. Although my friend and I had lived and traveled as missionaries through many countries and considered ourselves seasoned travelers, it was a new experience for my younger daughter.

Our plane arrived in London, where we spent one day sightseeing and trying to overcome jet lag. Then we jumped on a train that took us north, almost to the border of Scotland, to the Lake District, where we would spend several days. Our first day found us hiking all over the hills of Grasmere, the home of poet William Wordsworth. It was truly one of the most beautiful places I had ever seen, and we enjoyed the perfect weather of a golden autumn day. We greeted the next morning with excited anticipation of the same. However, when we checked out of our bed-and-breakfast, with suitcases in tow, we stepped into cold, drizzling rain and foggy mists.

With much difficulty, we crammed into a cab and asked our driver to take us to a place where we could store our luggage and handbags until we would take a train later that afternoon. In the meantime, we planned to ride a boat across a lake to the tiny village of Sawrey. We were running late, so we dropped off our bags and rushed to the lakeside dock, accidentally splashing through the puddles along the way. We boarded a tiny white fishing boat that was bouncing up and down furiously in the stormy waters. I knew we were in for a turbulent ride. Soaked and frozen by the pelting rain, we huddled together, teeth chattering, trying to keep warm. The foaming waves were so choppy, I wondered if we would make it across!

When we arrived at the other side, after the longest fifteen-minute ride, we pulled out our umbrellas in an attempt to shield ourselves from the rain. But the wind was blowing too hard, and our umbrellas flew upside down and inside out.

Despite the terrible weather, we were excited about our destination. Sawrey was a charming old English village. We headed slowly to Hill Top Farm, the quaint, delightful cottage that had been home to Beatrix Potter, the famous children's author. Through a small, crooked door we entered into her imaginative world, a welcome refuge from the stormy weather. Dark, polished paneled-wood covered the walls, and old fireplaces crackling with flames offered a bright contrast to the rain drumming against the windows of the bungalow. Tiny rabbit and mouse figurines lined shelves, soft pastel sketches decorated the walls, and inviting piles of old books fed our enjoyment of the haven where so many charming stories had come to life through Potter's pen. We cuddled happily in the warmth of the home, trying to dry out from our rainy adventure. After leaving, we grabbed a quick cup of tea to fend off the chill that threatened to creep over us again while we waited in the rain to board the boat and head back out across the choppy lake.

After we finally completed the return trip across the lake, we picked up our luggage and slogged half a mile through the constant soaking rain to the train station. By this time, we had all given up on our umbrellas and just dragged our bags along behind us.

Our train seemed a welcome haven from the cold, dreary day. We secured four seats together, settled ourselves and all our belongings, then spread out crusty bread; pungent cheddar cheese; and grapes for a picnic lunch on a drop-down table. Not long after we had finished eating, four surly people boarded the train, walked right to where we were seated, and said, "You're sitting in the wrong seats. Even though the tag doesn't say the seats are reserved, we reserved them. You'll have to move." Sure enough, the conductor agreed. We collected our coats and scarves, bag of food, suitcases, and shoulder bags and tried to navigate the crowd of impatient passengers. Although we managed to find other seats, we were all separated from each other by multiple rows.

I was tired and worn out, cold and wet, and a little irritated. It seemed as if the cold outside was seeping into my spirit. I tried to check on my daughters every once in a while to make sure they were okay, but mostly I just sat and watched the countryside drift by. After several hours, Sarah, my oldest daughter, shouted down to us from her seat toward the front, "Hurry! I just found out that our stop is the next one and there won't be much time to get off."

Once again, the four of us made a spectacle of ourselves as we exited the train, knocking about with all of our paraphernalia, moving as quickly as possible onto a train platform in an unfamiliar station amidst the black darkness of night. Again, we were met with a constant drizzle.

Our first obstacle was a two-story staircase to the street level, which we had to climb with all our heavy bags in tow. We made it to the top with great relief, but we could find no taxis. Our aim was to locate the bed-and-breakfast where we had reservations. Exhaustion poked its finger into our weary bodies, seeking to dishearten our little gang. Yet everyone maintained a good attitude. An hour later, we were still slogging through the mud and splashing through unavoidable puddles on cobblestone roads. Our jeans were soaked up to our knees, our hair was dripping wet, and our faces were all smudged with melting mascara.

My friend commented, "Joy, you are so mature for your age. I don't know of another thirteen-year-old who wouldn't be crying by this point. It's such a relief for all of us adults for you to carry your own weight!"

Joy seemed to hearten at her words, and we all plodded on in silent endurance. Finally, at nine o'clock, one and a half hours after we left the train station, we saw our bed-and-breakfast through the dim light of a streetlamp. We knocked and knocked, and finally we glimpsed a small light turn on at the back of the house. The door opened, and a charming, white-haired, lively man greeted us warmly with a deep English lilt.

"I thought you had decided not to come, and I had given up on you on such a miserable night." After we told him our story, he gasped and said, "Why, the train station is more than two miles from here. I can't believe you walked it in this pouring rain!"

As we entered the small living room, we spotted a large ceramic bowl of bright yellow bananas—a delectable feast to our growling stomachs. Our host noticed our eager eyes on the bowl. "How long has it been since you have eaten?" he asked.

"Eight hours!" was our reply in unison.

"Well, let me see what I can drum up. The girls who do the breakfast don't come until tomorrow, but I will see what I can do. You go change your clothes and meet me for a party!"

It is amazing how grateful one becomes for simple fare after slogging through a day of rain, cold, miles of walking, and growling stomachs! We gathered around a small antique table, surrounded by teapots, Victorian pictures of children and animals, and an eye-feast of collectibles of every kind.

A steaming pot of strong black coffee, a pile of freshly buttered toast served with whipped honey, bananas, and bowls of cereal became for us a victory banquet. Each morsel was delectable to our appreciative growling stomachs. The shared conversation as we crowded together, the laughing, antics, and stories so generously delivered by our charming host made a great memory for us. The immense relief of being out of the rain, in a warm, inviting room, painted our faces with smiles. Our bodies heaved sighs of contentment as we finally pattered up the stairs to bed.

Later, as I lay in a double bed with my daughter Joy snuggling next to me, I told her that she was amazing to have made it through such a day without complaining even once. "I'm so impressed that you could walk that far and carry your own bags and be so cheerful while knowing you were drenched to the bone and exhausted and hungry. I don't think many thirteen-year-olds would have done so well. It was difficult for *me*, and I've been traveling for more than thirty years. Then you made it until nine o'clock without a bite to eat. And you were very gracious to our host for his simple meal."

"Mom, I feel so proud of myself," she said. "It's like I passed a hard test and now I feel like I'm a real companion to all the adults. I was thinking about how much more grateful I was for cereal and fruit than if I had a five-course meal prepared by a great chef on a normal day. We shared a great adventure, and I proved to myself that I wasn't just a little girl anymore. Even your friend told me that she didn't know a single teenager who could have done so well. I think this might be my favorite memory of the trip so far!"

What an amazing attitude. And how well she put into practice the apostle James's words: "Consider it all joy, my brethren, when you encounter various trials, knowing that the testing of your faith produces endurance. And let endurance have its perfect result, so that you may be perfect and complete, lacking in nothing" (James 1:2–4).

A SURPRISING SOURCE OF JOY

Although I've read and heard those verses my whole life, I'd never really focused on the joy aspect of enduring trials. But recently I read the verses again and thought, *Here is another "backward" verse!*

I have to admit that in light of many difficult trials in my life, the thought of more trials tends to fill me not with joy but with dread and fear. Life has been so much harder than I ever thought it would be as a child! Yet James makes it sound as if I am supposed to gut it up, put a smile on my face, and act happy.

Wanting to better understand this passage, I sought help from Bible commentaries. I discovered a whole different meaning. In this context, the reference to trials suggests the idea of a contest. In the last chapter, we talked about the Lord's discipline. These verses focus more on developing internal righteousness and character. The testing James referred to is more of a practice and exercise of skill and strength, an external ability.

In other words, we may make a commitment in our hearts to love Jesus and to follow him, but there come contests, so to speak, in our lives in which we have the opportunity to show and to prove the reality of our faith by our actions and our behavior. Only then is our faith worth something, and only then do we reap the benefit of our faith. When we pass through these trials, they become a source of joy. It is our greatest opportunity to serve God with solid faith, loyal love, and generous humility.

This is just what Joy experienced. The youngest of four children, always the baby to everyone else, she was constantly striving to live up to the expectations of her older siblings. She didn't want to be treated like a child, and on the trip, when she was confronted by the stress and trials of our journey, she acted in a mature way: she carried her suitcase without complaint, she handled her weariness and hunger, she kept going even when she was exhausted. She proved that she was indeed equal to an adult in this situation, and even *better* than some adults! It gave her a real sense of affirmation to prove herself—to have "passed the test" in our eyes and in hers.

Thinking back to that day as I focused on these verses through the lens of joy, I was able to capture some of God's point of view toward our temporary life in this world. I could look upon my own past trials and see how they led to a deep, abiding joy in my life.

God places training tests in our lives to allow us to exhibit our true character and skill. For a pianist who practices diligently for many years, for instance, a recital gives him the opportunity to show his skill and competence. And at the end, he senses a deep satisfaction in having performed well. The recital is the "test."

My twenty-year-old son, Nathan, recently communicated the same idea to me. He said "Mom, if a boxer trains to be an athlete his whole life and never has a chance to test his strength in the ring, it would make his training seem so pointless and empty. I feel like the boxer who has been training. I want my opportunity to go into the ring of life—to attempt to test my training and strength in a real arena."

But though James was not talking about piano recitals or boxing matches, he was talking about the real trials of life, the "hard" stuff. And in these trials, we show what we are really made of, how strong and skillful at living for Christ we have become.

For me, the hard stuff started when I was a young single woman. Trying to figure out how to meet a "good" guy and foray through the obstacle course of dating, while keeping my morality intact, was sometimes disheartening. Next, my surprise came as a young missionary overseas. I thought a person who was committed enough to move overseas must be a very spiritual person. Yet when I joined my mission team, I found these "spiritual giants" struggled with the same self-centered, petty personality issues that my old friends in America struggled with—only we didn't have as many support systems to buoy us up.

The next arena of challenge was marriage. When Clay and I got married, we brought with us a lot of emotional baggage from our less-than-perfect backgrounds. We were immature, self-centered, and had personalities so different that we often rubbed each other the wrong way. Many of the relational habits we had developed were not healthy. And although we were committed Christians, still we hit some difficult times of conflict through the years.

I was a passionate, relational, affectionate dreamer. I hate to say it, but I was confident that my "ways" were quite spiritual. Clay was introverted, rational, organized, practical, and *also* convinced that his way of seeing life was right. Those times of darkness were the tests we had to pass: Would we remain committed to each other in spite of our differences? Did I understand that my loyalty to Clay, even when I felt distant, was an issue of faith between God and me? Would I, for the sake of my love and commitment to Christ, commit to serve Clay and act out of unconditional love?

Somewhere during those dark times I realized that God is not so much concerned with my immediate gratification as he is with the development of my soul. I had a choice to trust God with my loneliness as I waited for marriage, to trust God while learning to work with, love, and serve my committed but normal and all-too-human team members. I had a choice to trust God while hoping for a "Cinderella" marriage yet learning that it takes work to build intimacy, to nurture and cultivate a life-giving and loving environment in our home. Through each of these situations, God led me to understand more deeply and clearly the sacrifice of love, the power of unconditional acceptance and commitment that also defines God's love for me. Marriage was one of the biggest testing grounds for me.

Clay, too, had choices to make. He saw how critical my attitude was and how self-righteous I could be. Either he could give in to his anger and frustration, blasting me with the reality of my immaturity and acting resentfully toward me, or he could be faithful to God and patient with me.

Of course, neither of us always responded to these tests perfectly. Too often we chose paths that didn't draw us closer to each other or to God. But now, having practiced faithfulness through the trials of those many seasons, our love is deep and sure. Now that I am more aware of my sin, I can't believe Clay put up with me! But having lived together through years of babies, moves, illnesses, catastrophes, financial pressures, and temptations, our love is all the more precious and of great value. It has become a treasure. I find deep, fulfilling joy in knowing that we have made it through and in the process brought so much more worth to the marriage commitment of our lives.

I understand more how blessed we are to have had the opportunity to be loyal to God and to have passed the test. On this side of it, my heart is filled with great joy. I have such relief to know that I don't have to deal with the regret of giving up too soon in the battle.

> Strength is born in the deep silence of
> long-suffering hearts; not amidst joy.
>
> FELICIA HEMANS

YOUR PATH ISN'T MY PATH

God has designed us to be satisfied by work and accomplishment, and indeed accomplishment in kingdom work—the "tough" stuff—is a satisfaction that cannot be taken away. So the question of our lives is not, "Will we have tests?" Instead the question becomes, "How will we respond to the tests life brings?"

As a young woman, I told God I wanted to be his servant and to be used greatly in this world. It has been in living faithfully through countless tests that God has fit me for ministry. Having struggled through the trials of life has made me much better suited to connect with a broad range of women. My heart is more compassionate because I have been humbled and tested through many roles of life—as a single woman, a married woman, a mother, a working woman, a woman tempted to depression, a woman with conflict from family, a woman with health issues and financial stresses. These tests exercised my spiritual muscles and increased my capacity to work. And yes, now I am grateful for all the tests because they brought joy.

Of course, we each will face different tests in our lives. When I was younger, my best friend longed to get married, take care of children, and be domestic. It was what she most wanted. Yet she ended up being single and alone for her whole life. But because she responded to God's tests over many years by saying, as Mary did, "May it be done to me according to your word" (Luke 1:38) and sought to live out her life faithfully, *just as it was*, she became one of the most loving, life-giving, mature people I know.

And yet I, who really had never longed to have children, got married and had four. I have probably learned more from the Lord about joy in the midst of trials by being a parent than in any other role. It is what I needed to become the woman he wanted me to be. And it's taken years to get there! God doesn't grow us in character and joy quickly. He has a long-term perspective for me. He sees the training process over a period of years and is always seeking to move me ahead in my character.

Often it seems we would rather have another life—any life—than our own. Somehow we think if we lived a different life, it would be easier for us to grow in faithfulness and spiritual character. Yet it is in accepting today with all of its issues, in accepting God's will and training grounds that we learn the secret of joy in his presence. It is in being faithful to our own set of tests that we become mature and fitted for the ministry he has called each of us to accomplish. If we aspire to be a general, so to speak, spiritually, then we must first pass the training and tests of life as a private!

Other friends have lived through the devastation of divorce, personal rejection, financial losses, illnesses. Whether it is dealing with a prodigal child, an unfaithful spouse, an angry parent, unjust accusations, the loss of a job, or any other kind of trial, we always have a choice to endure with strength or capitulate to the darkness of our souls.

Certainly, most of us would not choose any of the stresses that a fallen world brings our way. But that is exactly why Jesus said, "In the world you have tribulation, but take courage; I have overcome the world" (John 16:33). He knew that this world, imperfect and in rebellion to God, would be very difficult. Yet he promised to be with us!

THE JOY OF RESISTING COMPROMISE

We each will face a variety of tests in different areas of life. A single adult looking for a spouse has a choice of compromising her morals or waiting patiently for God's provision. Someone who has been hurt or rejected in a group of Christians is tested in her ability to forgive and give grace rather than become bitter. A tragedy like a car accident or fire tests whether we will believe in God's goodness or shake our fist at him with accusations of injustice or indifference. Parents face the test of whether to pursue our own rights and interests or give up personal time and priorities in order to invest in training our children and learning what it means to be a servant leader.

As a mother, I felt God leading me to give up my time and my career in order to be available to actively pursue the well-being of my children and to direct the training of their souls. This was the puzzle he gave me to solve. Three out of four of my children were asthmatics, and one had a learning disability that created havoc and mystery for us. I had to be available to my family through seventeen moves because of our commitment to international ministry, which involved long bouts of loneliness for me. I had to give my time to train my immature children over and over and over again through the long process of taking them from infancy to adulthood. Because I had never really been prepared to do housework and to take care of children (I almost never baby-sat in my whole life and was the youngest and only girl in my family), mothering and home-making were things I had to learn over a period of time. Sometimes I would pass these tests well, and sometimes I would fail. But it was a string of tests that trained me and shaped me to become mature over a period of time. Similarly, it took years and years to move my children from babyhood and self-absorption to the emotional, mental, spiritual, and physical maturity of young adults.

Choices to serve them through the beauty of my home and to provide emotional and academic excellence and healthy meals never came easy for me. Yet this became my daily training ground for growing in and serving Christ. I felt I needed to give them my best because Christ values all children, and these particular children were entrusted into my hands. The outcome of this *very* long test is that now I have seen God's faithfulness built into their lives, and it has become a foundation for my ministry.

Trials are rarely over quickly, and God does not work on our preferred timetable. As I noted before, he is more committed to the process of our growth than to our immediate gratification. As we submit to his will, we will find that we were made or suited to find joy in that place.

I encountered many dark hours along the way as I sought to figure out just what he wanted me to do. Many times I raised my children without family or support systems. Often, I would wonder if I was just wasting my time and effort, which could be better used somewhere else. Now, though, I am filled with great joy as I glean some satisfying results. But even beyond the joy, a peace resides within me from having endured all the years and in having seen God work. I have a confidence that God is good, a fulfillment that came through seeing the fruit of my labor and faith. I experience freedom and peace, which I always longed for when I was young and idealistic.

Our integrity as people of God will come by walking the path that he has given to us. We will not have this fulfillment, satisfaction, or joy if we compromise our ideals and resist the tests that God puts in our pathway.

CHOICES AMID A SELF-GRATIFYING WORLD

The key to joy in the midst of trials is in knowing and believing that God is always good. Always.

I must remember and choose to believe that he is working even when I can't see him; that this test is the work of my life—my opportunity to have a testimony or story of his faithfulness. Then each day, each minute, I must turn my heart toward praise, thanksgiving, and rest, knowing that God is producing in me the character of Christ.

Worrying and fretting just squeeze out joy. I can't live in both worlds at once—the peace of Christ and the worry of the world—so I must turn my back on fear or dread and turn my face toward his promises as I wait in the knowledge of his grace.

One of the problems, however, when it comes to these trials of faith is that, in a world where the rules of life are based on foolish values and false standards, we have forgotten the wisdom of God. No longer do we value hard work, diligence, and perseverance, as was affirmed by God in Genesis before the Fall. Instead we value leisure time, vacations, and entertainment. If we confront a problem in marriage, instead of serving our spouse, we want to have our own needs met and give in to no-fault divorce. We want quick fixes to children's needs—fast food is easier than cooking a real meal and washing dishes. Turning on the TV is an easier option for entertaining children than taking them outside to play, or sitting down to read a book, or playing a game with them. If we don't like one job, it is easier just to quit than to work through the problems. An unwanted pregnancy is more easily taken care of by an abortion than by taking responsibility for the consequences of sex and being committed to raising and embracing a baby. Ours is not a culture that values tests but one that values the ease of life.

Consequently, we deprive human beings of the dignity that comes from exhibiting strength of character. We were created with abundant capacities to be strong, heroic, artistic, intelligent, and excellent. Because we were made in God's image, we are most satisfied and fulfilled when we have the opportunity to practice and grow in these excellent attributes.

If we meet all the wants of a little baby and never allow it to grow, it becomes a pathetic, whiny, weak-willed child. Yet when a child is given responsibility a little at a time amid instruction and training, the child is much more likely to be content and feel a proper sense of his own importance. In a similar way, God's children are given training, tests, and responsibility so that we will also grow strong. As a Father, God is always a trainer of character. He will not leave us alone—he is an engaged Father, always mindful of our future well-being and character.

> Although the world is full of suffering, it is full also of the overcoming of it.... We could never learn to be brave and patient, if there were only joy in the world.
>
> HELEN KELLER

THE TRUE CONTEST

Since the beginning, Satan has tempted man to be disloyal to God, his Creator; he has vied for our allegiance. The Old Testament book of Job is an example of this. Satan, who roams to and fro through the whole earth, seeking whom he may devour, was searching for another human being to test—to see if he could cause him to curse God and turn away from him. Satan said that Job followed God only because his life was so blessed. But God had seen into Job's heart. He knew that Job was a devoted follower. So Satan threw every possible temptation and trial Job's way to see if he could make him hate and renounce God. But it was to God's great glory that Job passed the test—he stayed faithful to the Lord his God.

Job's story of testing has become a model for us all on how to walk with God. Job must have experienced, in the end, everlasting joy in knowing that he had passed the test, that he'd seized the opportunity to show God's faithfulness, and that he'd come through with a story for all eternity of *his* faithfulness to God.

This is the true contest that has taken place since the beginning of time. Those who remain loyal to God and obey his will have a place in history where their story of faithfulness will be told throughout all generations. These tests are our opportunities to exhibit to God and to the world the integrity of our faith in him and our commitment to do his will, just like all of those in the Hebrews hall of fame (Hebrews 11). Our tests present each of us with the prospect to be found on God's side, to be counted among those who do not shrink back but stand firm in faith and character.

Great joy comes in the freedom of having passed through difficult seasons and having seen his faithfulness along the way. I feel that I am more the person I want to be *because* of the many tests of my life. God has shared with me his wisdom along the way. He has shown me that with him I am stronger and more capable of accomplishing more things in life than I ever would have imagined.

Because of these truths, I can now greet other tests with more peace and grace, knowing that they can compel me to look more longingly toward heaven and can give me a deeper love and appreciation for my Father and his unconditional love to me, his child. Even though I don't desire trials, I can enter into them in anticipation of how they can become my greatest accomplishments.

Joy, then, comes in embracing the opportunity to be a part of his world of righteousness and preparing to live with him in that kingdom for eternity. Joy comes in following where he leads me, choosing to believe that his way is good and that he works according to his will. I quench this joy when I resist him and fight against the dance he is trying to teach me. I experience the grace of the dance when I follow his direction and his lead, even when it seems to be the opposite of what I might have done.

To grow in this joy, I have to move where he leads. When dancers attempt to turn in different directions, there is no beauty, no synchronizing of movement. But when they learn to read each other's movements and move as one body, there is a beauty, a grace, and a skill of step that grants the joy of unity and elegance to the dance.

Finding *Your* Rhythm in God's Joy

1. James told us to "Consider it all joy…when you encounter various trials, knowing that the testing of your faith produces endurance" (James 1:2–3). List the trials that you are experiencing right now.

   How does God want you to pass the test of these particular trials?

   What attitude do you need to change or cultivate?

2. Psalm 103:8 says, "The LORD is compassionate and gracious, slow to anger and abounding in lovingkindness." Is this how you picture God, even in the midst of your trials?

   How do you need to change your perception of him in order to receive his compassion, grace, and generous lovingkindness?

3. Paul wrote in 2 Timothy 3:1–3: "But realize this, that in the last days difficult times will come. For men will be lovers of self, lovers of money, boastful, arrogant, revilers, disobedient to parents, ungrateful, unholy, unloving, irreconcilable, malicious gossips, without self-control, brutal, haters of good."

   How does this apply to our culture?

How does culture with its messages distract us from God's ways for us, to work hard and to endure with grace in order to develop character?

What do you need to do to embrace God's ways so that you will find joy as you "dance these steps with him"?

Dear heavenly Father,

You are a good father and committed to excellence in my life. Open my eyes that I may see what is really taking place in my heart. Help me to be committed to the long-term pathway of facing my tests and trials with strength and the knowledge that it is in my every day where greatness of soul is being shaped. Help me to learn to accept with joy the life you have given to me. I love you, Lord. In Jesus' name I come.

Five

Reveling in God's Melody of Joy

Slouched down wearily in my leather seat in a crowded railway car, I was being gently rocked to sleep by the rhythmic back-and-forth swaying of the old train as it clattered across the Polish countryside. The mesmerizing *clickety-clack* of the wheels moving mile by mile reminded me of a squeaky rocker my father used to ease me into dreamland as a youngster. He would sing to me as I slowly gave way to sleep, enjoying the swaying movement of the rocker.

The memory of those peaceful interludes and the cadence of the moving train soothed my weary spirit and body. I was returning from a student conference in the southern mountains where I had been teaching and counseling college students all weekend. It had left me drained, lonely, and depleted. Working through translators for each message was a slow, tedious process. As a twenty-four-year-old American woman in the late 1970s, I felt the cultural distance between me and these youth who had grown up under a suppressive Communist government. The lack of religious freedom made these students eager to know about God, Jesus, and a kingdom in heaven where they would be free and blessed by the One who made them. And while I was excited to share with them, I was worn out from trying to communicate past the language barriers. Exhaustion tended to exaggerate the cultural differences. A sense of isolation dogged me as I struggled to understand even a portion of the things they were saying.

As I rode in the train car, I wondered if I would ever *not* be lonely. My soul felt like a desolate island in the sea of so many foreign elements. Question marks filled my brain in pondering my future. *Will I be able to handle this work? Did I hear God right in becoming a missionary?* These were the moments when I longed for the security and stability of marriage. Yet I also enjoyed the adrenaline surge of being on an adventure alone as a single woman in this country, doing God's business and experiencing new opportunities and interesting people every day. My thoughts went back and forth so much that I was feeling schizophrenic!

The train curved around a bend in the track. Abruptly I saw displayed out my window thousands upon thousands of bright red poppies growing wild in the rural countryside and swaying gently in the wind. The elegant movement of scarlet blossoms swirling in the breezes gave the impression of a hundred ballerinas dancing across the stage of the horizon. I could almost hear the flowers singing as they played their enchanting melody over my soul. The sheer beauty of dancing flowers and the contrasting color of bright red framed in black and strewn amongst the spring green of the fields was stunning. I wondered how many years it had taken for these beautiful flowers to be planted so that there would be so many everywhere. My soul began to swell with happiness just to behold such an unusual sight, and my mood lightened as I savored the moment.

I imagined the invisible hand of God intentionally spreading seed generously over the many fields as he rambled through the countryside. Perhaps in a country that had seen so much division, war, and darkness for so many generations, God intentionally ordained for there still to be a picture of his beauty, creation, and life to comfort those who would see it. His gracious gift would draw their hearts, as it did mine, to thoughts of the Artist of such beauty.

I have never forgotten that moment, though more than thirty years have passed. The impression of beauty picked me up emotionally, spiritually, and mentally and made me realize how present God is in my life every day through what he has created. Even more, I realized that he created it for my joy and the joy of all who would open their eyes to its grandeur. To encounter such beauty was to encounter the invading presence of God.

Crystal clear in my memory reside many such times when something unexpected broke into an ordinary moment to capture my attention and to bring utter delight or amazement or soul-deep awe.

The more I study the character of God, the more I see that God is not a kill-joy grump. Rather, in some ways, he is wild, whimsical, transcendent, and like a playful dancer, weaving steps and songs into the pattern of our days. As the author of humor, delight, tastes, sounds, feelings, touch, and affection, he tucks beauty along our pathway to show us more of his artistry.

God's personality is to be a provider of beauty as the very expression of his nature.

> The earth was formless and void, and darkness was over the surface of the deep, and the Spirit of God was moving over the surface of the waters. Then God said, "Let there be light"; and there was light.
>
> GENESIS 1:2–3

GOD IS OUT OF THE BOX!

One cold, snowy winter's day, one of my children was drinking a cup of hot chocolate in our kitchen. She said, "I'm so glad our God is out of the box in our home!"

"What do you mean?" I asked.

"Well, a lot of people we know act like God is mad a lot and mainly concerned with us knowing all the right answers and doing lots of good work and keeping all the rules. But our God is the One who created chili peppers for fajitas, Celtic music to dance to, puppy dogs to be snuggled, jokes for giggling, and stars to enjoy when we sleep out on the deck. We enjoy him and what he made. We don't just work for him—that's what I mean."

I was so glad that is what my child perceived in our home—a personal creator-God, filled with infinite ideas of ways to fill our world with things to enjoy.

Many Christians tend to defend fervently their theological underpinnings and argue rigorously the tenets of doctrine. Yet often I have observed that in choosing to live only in a cerebral world of "what I know intellectually about God," they miss so much of his personality and nature, which can be observed through his role as the Artist.

Because we live in an isolated, somewhat cerebral time, we define our worth by what we know or what kind of a degree we have or by the work we accomplish. Our spirituality is often expressed by the theological philosophy we claim—charismatic or reformed or Baptist or Catholic. Data, facts, and knowledge as reflected by scores on academic tests are often the measure of a person's worth. Life is fast-paced, efficient, impersonal. We regularly shut God out of our lives to center our attention on worldly achievement and then wonder where he has gone.

Such an overemphasis on the academic determines that a relationship with God will be dryly intellectual but obviously absent of feeling and delight. It would be like writing or defending a long treatise on the role of a father, his character, and the history of fatherhood—separate from relating personally and intimately with him. No "report on fatherhood" would ever satisfy our need to experience life with an actual father, the life that comes from engaging in the personality, friendship, and companionship of a real live person.

God intended that we become witnesses of his beauty, design, color, and pleasure so that we could gain a more intimate, real, and personal knowledge of him. God does not want to be just a thought to know, but a personally engaging friend and Father whose relationship with us is filled with memory, delight, and moments to be experienced and enjoyed.

As I began to write this chapter, I tried to remember other memories of times in which I was astonished by a sense of his indefinable beauty. Those thoughts quieted and comforted me with awe. A glorious sunrise on a cold beach in Florida during a getaway with friends in college and how the spectacular, quiet moments of light spilled into the darkness. A glowing full moon suspended in the cloudless sky one evening minutes before a lunar eclipse. Snow crystals shimmering in the early morning as I opened my eyes from sleep to observe the first snowfall of the winter in our new Colorado home. A triple rainbow majestically filling the rain-cleansed sky at the tail of a storm, which seemed to flow completely from the east horizon to the west horizon. Five deer bucks idling in our front yard in the late afternoon sun, making a feast on our summer grass, as I, unnoticed, sipped a cup of tea on our porch.

These thoughts led me to recognize other opportunities for joy that I experience every day but often neglect to see as a part of God's personality and imagination invading the moments of my life.

> Rejoice in the Lord always; again I will say, rejoice!
>
> PHILIPPIANS 4:4

FOOD FOR THOUGHT

As I continued to relive memories of God's creative personality, I realized many had to do with food! Sitting on a café patio one cool summer's night and indulging in spicy chicken and beef fajitas with cheese and guacamole; hot chocolate fudge cake with whipped cream at a family birthday event; hot tea with fresh, warm scones, clotted cream, and jam at a friend's home; apple pie fresh from the oven, baked after picking the apples from an orchard. Much of my pleasure in life comes from the experiences I receive through my senses, which God gave me and which God delights in satisfying.

Even now these and many other pictures arrest me with a beauty that transcends my normal world. Each picture speaks of an Artist who paints with a palette of color, taking care to design his creations with movement and life. Yet, often I don't think of these things as gifts from the One who made them. I just take them for granted as a part of my material world.

But in reality, God made such moments to bring tangible pleasure to my life. Each day is filled with sense-invigorating pleasures: eating at least three meals a day, imbibing countless warm cups of coffee and tea, falling into my comfy bed after kissing my children good night, listening to music every day on my iPod and swaying and pulsating to the rhythm of the songs, enjoying the intimate embrace of my husband. All of these

I was created to enjoy so that my life would not be dull and lifeless as cardboard.

What an amazing, charming, wonderful God, that he would go to such detail to bring delight to so many moments of my life. To understand him as the source of these pleasures and to have a grateful heart for bringing such dimension to my days fills me with humble appreciation. How often I have ignored his presence in these small everyday happenings, yet how careful he was to design my life to be so enjoyable. Rather than serving as the backdrop for "real life," such scenes should bring to the foreground of my mind the obvious reality of God, making me feel part of something bigger than myself. God designed it so.

THE WITNESS OF CREATION

I have learned that one of my most important areas of stewardship is to cultivate a personal, inspirational, and intimate knowledge of God. In Romans 1:20, Paul told us that, "Since the creation of the world His [God's] invisible attributes, His eternal power and divine nature, have been clearly seen, being understood through what has been made." This means that through creation we can discover his invisible attributes: what God is like, his eternal power, the strength of his might from eternity past until eternity future, the very nature of his personality. His signature is on everything he has made! And he made all of these pleasures as a love gift to us that we might perceive him more clearly.

In other words, if I want to know what God is like—if I want to see a visible reflection of his nature—then one of the best and most complete teachers is nature, the platform of his original work. Through nature, we observe that ours is a God of variety. Think about the plethora of his creation. Countless colors, shapes, personalities, and sounds. Insects, fish, birds, puppies, hippos, and penguins. Textures soft, hard, rough, jagged. Temperatures icy cold and steaming hot. Designs of stripes, polka dots, circles, squares, rectangles. Dimensions immense and tiny, fragile and powerful. We can listen to sounds and learn that God is musical: birds chirping, bees buzzing, leaves chattering in the wind, cows mooing. He even had angels singing at his birth. We observe that he is orderly by looking at the design of a cell or noting the predictability of a sunrise and sunset or recognizing the constancy of the seasons. We observe his power through storms, waterfalls, and beasts.

God has inscribed a book about himself, and we can read it by paying attention to the things that are in our lives every day: our yards, the storms, the night sky, the sea. His imprint is *everywhere*.

The key to enjoying God in every moment of these daily pleasures is to open the eyes of my mind to see and to appreciate what he has given. A thankful heart galvanizes the connection between my God and me.

Recently, one of my sons returned home after spending a year at a school in New York City. The typical preparations we make for a loved one's returning include drawing "I love you" signs and posting them all over the house and the front door, baking a batch of homemade chocolate chip cookies, cleaning the house, lighting candles, putting on favorite music, and serving a feast of the returnee's choosing. Though my son had experienced these meals and celebrations so many times before, he cherished them all the more after having been away for a year. At the end of the evening, he said, "Mom, you can't imagine how thankful I am to be home and how blessed I am to have your great cooking again. Thanks so much for going to the trouble. I appreciated every moment of our time together tonight."

My pleasure in having worked so hard to welcome him increased immeasurably because of the appreciation he expressed. I felt closer to him, and because his love for me was more on a reciprocal level, we have experienced more mutual sharing and closeness as one adult to another instead of just the immature love he gave as a youngster. Now that he has grown up and doesn't take home for granted, he gives a worthier praise.

Similarly, when we really see that God is a wonderful Provider and has gone to great lengths to make our earthly home pleasurable, we will appreciate him more and our hearts will be lifted to thank him. It is when we come to see what he has given that we begin to be mature. It is when we understand that God's gifts are with consideration of our truest needs—for love, beauty, purpose, belonging—instead of for our selfish gratification, material possessions, ownership. When we are humble and appreciative of who he really is, then we move down the road to a more foundational intimacy with him. But without a heart of thanksgiving, in which we recognize his chosen gifts, our joy will not be full.

A thing of beauty is a joy for ever.

JOHN KEATS

FRIENDSHIP WITH GOD

When two people become intimate friends, it happens because they have grown to love each other by sharing life together. They know each other's personality, laugh at the same jokes, enjoy the same experiences, and mutually express appreciation for the relationship. They share common values and articulate love and enjoyment to each other in a variety of ways. Similarly, two lovers grow in their attraction and fondness of each other by spending time together, having fun, sharing thoughts and ideas, getting to know each other, needing each other, and appreciating and being grateful for each other.

This is the kind of friendship God intends for us to enjoy with him: sharing in all the experiences of life together, talking to him throughout the day, appreciating the different pleasures and blessings he sprinkles along our path. What we experience in our human relationships is only a small shadow of what he meant for us to experience with him every day.

If we were made for relationship, love, intimacy, and community with God—our ultimate friend and provider of all of the pleasurable moments—then it would be logical that our joy in the spiritual realm would depend not just on our mental knowledge or assent to God's existence but on our pleasure in knowing him as a friend, lover, Father, and companion. What do we know of God's personality? his pleasure? his attitude toward fun and adventure, laughter and joy? Isn't it true that often, when religious people live by law and works, they feel guilty enjoying life and experiencing pleasure? We sometimes live as if God is so much more concerned about our works and deeds and may even believe that he is stern and not pleased with us if we are silly, happy, or enjoying life.

How frustrating it must be to God to know that we sometimes picture him as a grumpy old man only interested in our perfect behavior, ready at any moment to spoil our fun and to slap us with harsh discipline the moment we fail, and who wants us always to be quiet and well-behaved. I am convinced that God meant for us to regularly experience pleasure and delight, laughter, and pure, unadulterated joy. But in order for these to be an integral part of a very real relationship with him, we need to find him in beauty and pleasure in the minute places and details of our lives.

Joy is not just a word to be understood or a spiritual concept to be studied. No! Joy is a depth of feeling to be experienced, based on real pleasure and bliss, which God created us to revel in, to respond to, and to enjoy. If we separate God from the physical world where we live and breathe, then we will not have the fullness of joy he intended us to have and to experience.

> Where were you when I laid the foundation of the earth?
> Tell Me, if you have understanding, who set its
> measurements? Since you know. Or who stretched
> the line on it? On what were its bases sunk? Or who laid
> its cornerstone, when the morning stars sang together
> and all the sons of God shouted for joy?
>
> JOB 38:4-7

GOD AT WORK

When Job pondered the "unanswerables" of his life, his trials, the unjust remarks of his friends, the justice of God, the sadness of losing his children and his health and all that he had, he railed at the unfairness. He was unaware that he was caught in a holy battle for allegiance raging in heaven between Satan and God. He was also not aware of the fact that Satan was the one who had devastated his life (Job 1:12). Satan had been "roaming about on the earth" (verse 7) and seeking whom he could devour, as Peter reminded us in 1 Peter 5:8 ("Be on the alert. Your adversary, the devil, prowls around like a roaring lion, seeking someone to devour.").

This is a graphic picture of the trials we were speaking of in chapter 4. Satan did not believe that Job would stay loyal to God, and yet in every temptation Job held fast to God's promise. But in the thick of the struggles, when Job questioned God, God asked *him* a question hoping to arouse his sensibilities.

Where were you when I laid the foundation of the earth?
Tell Me, if you have understanding,
Who set its measurements? Since you know.
Or who stretched the line on it?
On what were its bases sunk?
Or who laid its cornerstone,
When the morning stars sang together
And all the sons of God shouted for joy? (Job 38:4–7)

Here is a picture of God in the midst of creating the world, the Artist throwing into place the universe. It must have been the most extraordinary event in time—to see the universe literally coming into place. The response was that the stars sang (yes, even music came from God's hand). Imagine a choir of stars performing a concert for God's glory! And the sons of God shouted for joy. They were excited and stirred up. They didn't just say joyful words; they were ecstatic and spontaneous. *Wow! Hurrah! Amazing! Cool!* They shouted for *joy.* The beauty of creation, at the beginning of its history, required a spontaneous response of joyful, loud, out-of-control shouting.

I will never forget one occasion when I felt overwhelmed in nature, certain I was in the presence of a fun, dancing, delightful—and delighted—God. I was in Australia speaking to several groups. At around 5:00 a.m. I awakened to what almost seemed like a dream. Outside my window, birds were cawing, whistling, and singing to one another; insects were chirping and buzzing; and mysterious animals—I knew not what—were hooting and humming.

My daughter and I dressed quickly to walk outside and take it all in. As we stepped out onto the country road in front of our bed-and-breakfast, I was overwhelmed with the celebration of life and the symphony of sound that surrounded us. Gigantic butterflies were gently

swaying in the breezes; brilliantly colored flowers and bushes were blooming and sending out sweet scents; parrots and cockatoos were flying
around in the high trees. And not far away from us stood an animal leaning on its back legs.

My daughter and I sputtered as we both exclaimed, "Look at that
thing in the road! It's a, uh, um, I don't know. It's too small to be a kan-
garoo. Isn't it sweet? And funny? What is it?" As if on cue, it jumped
away. We found out later it was a wallaby.

It seemed to me that every point in sight vibrated with movement
and flying and chirping, and all was ablaze with color. The warm life of
the creatures and plants was almost palpable. It gave new meaning to
Genesis 1, when God created the earth. Even though I had never encountered this abundance before, it didn't mean it didn't exist. It always existed
like this through the centuries, but once I experienced it, it became a part
of me. It awakened a place in my soul that was longing to be stirred. This
gave me a hilarious sense of fun and adventure to explore such a foreign
but delightfully sensual place. I had a new venue for experiencing life, for
enjoying eye pleasure, ear pleasure, tactile pleasure.

What Isolates Us from God

Evident in this experience was the fact that there must have been a much
more profound substantiation of God's handiwork in creation long, long
ago, when the world was untouched by pollution, industrialization, the
forming of large cities, and population. I am not just talking about envi-
ronmental issues; I was truly astounded at this new world that always
existed and yet that I had never experienced. It made me feel as if God
had secret places and powers that he would exhibit throughout the universe as an expression of spontaneous creativity, just as his Artist nature
demands.

It dawned on me that if this was so pleasing to me somewhere deep inside, then he must have meant for us to experience deep, gratifying delight and joy that we somehow miss out on in our contemporary world. Perhaps the more isolated we are from nature, the more isolated we will feel from God, and so we remove ourselves from one of his most personal gifts to bring us joy.

This indeed gave real meaning to God's question to Job. In other words, "Job, when you consider that my hand made the marvels of nature, which because of the grandeur called forth a spontaneous cheering and song, then you can know that I am beyond understanding. I am bigger than this isolated moment of pain on the earth. Job, in this you can know my eternal transcendence. You can know that I am the infinite, the Creator, your heavenly Father. I am above and beyond all of your finite mind's consideration of what you see in this moment. I am infinite in power, glory, beauty, and purpose. Let what you see comfort you—that I am above and beyond all of your present sufferings and limitations. Then you will be able to trust in the midst of difficulties, which you cannot yet understand."

I realized that in our time of history, living in the throes of a technological world where everyone rides in cars with closed windows and subways that speed along, when we stay inside our enclosed boxes (houses and apartments) to watch television and to play with our machines (computers and gaming devices), the creation of God is blocked out. Often, too, this kind of living produces isolation from real people.

For most of history, man was directly dependent on local agriculture. The productivity of a farmer in raising food, and the home gardens that provided daily sustenance, placed people in a more naturally God-dependent frame of mind. They were intrinsically connected to the earth for their prosperity.

Now, however, we just drive in our car to the local store, and food magically appears on the shelves, and we have removed God from the equation. Consequently, much that he intended us to know about himself, those things he wanted us to experience by being immersed in nature and what he made for our pleasure, has been hidden and suppressed by contemporary life. The intrinsic joy and comfort that comes from being enveloped in the beauty of nature is lost on us. We have hidden ourselves from one of the greatest sources of comfort and happiness that he designed just for us to enjoy.

As Paul wrote in Romans 1, God's creation in nature provides multitudes of examples of beauty that reveal countless lessons and impressions about our Creator. And we are without excuse because of the great evidence of God's existence through what he made. So when we stay in our air-conditioned cars or ride in underground subways, whizzing from activity to activity, and waste hours of time alone in front of a TV, we are separating ourselves from ample evidence of God's existence. And then we occasionally mutter under our breath in a lone moment, "Where are you, God? How come I can't feel your presence anymore?"

Time, or lack of time, is also at the heart of our problem. We are so occupied with our "duties" that we separate ourselves from the soul-pleasures that God created for us to enjoy. Because we are too busy working, we lack intimate relationships with the ultimate creations, human beings: our family, children, and friends. We don't know our neighbors or even the people in the church pew sitting next to us. We are masterful at succumbing and adjusting to such a dry, sawdust experience of life, all the while not knowing that he is still here—present in nature and as we rock a baby, hold a hand, share a meal and conversation.

To deny our souls this pleasure is like denying our bodies healthy food. Eventually our bodies will become unhealthy if we neglect them. So our souls will shrivel and die if they are not fed on the beauty, love, and delight of life that God created.

Satan would love for us to block out the miraculous evidence of God's creative genius, which speaks volumes to us of his constant presence and reality. To resist this temptation, we must remove those things in our lives and schedules that put blinders on our souls' eyes. We must engage with his very present, physical reality through what he has created us to observe every day. What might this require of you? Change your schedule. Plan time to walk outside, plant a garden, listen to the rain on the roof, picnic outside in the spring.

RESTORING LIFE TO OUR SOULS

Hope for the redemption of our dead souls springs forth even as we look to nature for our lessons. I find, though, that the season of spring has become to me the most accurate picture of what happens to my soul as I watch for signs of our personal creator God.

The winter season reflects the death of nature. The leaves have fallen off seemingly dead trees, the fruit of the ground has disappeared, the cold storms of snow and rain prevail against our windowpanes. Yet in this dried out and lifeless landscape, suddenly green shoots begin to come up through the hard, cold ground; blossoms miraculously begin to sprout with color. Wonder fills our souls to see the life of God literally "springing forth" from the seeming death of winter—such a picture of resurrection and life power that cannot be stopped or contained.

Joy calls forth in me and in my weary soul a desire to move from the winter of separation from God's delight to the verdant life of his resurrection power springing forth inside of me as I see his hand, his love, his beauty present in my life every day. Even as the little boy in the Polish park stopped to enjoy and dance among the falling spring blossoms, so we must *choose* to stop and experience and enjoy God's personality. We must resolve to have this as a priority so that when the opportunity arises, we are ready to spontaneously give attention to our friends and to our heavenly Father, who is so ready to delight and fill our souls. We cannot maintain life as usual, with all the things that scream for our attention, and still see his beauty and hear his voice.

When I pick a bouquet of flowers and arrange them on a table, or provide a picnic with freshly baked bread and slices of cold peaches, or initiate a moonlit hike, I am placing myself and my friends or children in the pathway of God so that they might also marvel at what he has made and be drawn to his greatness. When I initiate a once-a-month gathering in my home and light candles, turn on delightful music, place boughs of tree blossoms or honeysuckle in a vase on my table, I provide an atmosphere where his presence and joy is embodied in fellowship. I build friendships and put myself in the company of people who extend to me God's love and affirmation.

When we arrange life, time, and opportunities for precious people in our lives to grow to understand, know, and experience the beauty that God so generously provided for us to enjoy, then we become co-creators, so to speak, in the Spirit of Christ who lives in and through us. And so the dance of life becomes for us more elegant, great, and joyful because we have begun to hear his music all around us. We have learned to affirm his reality and his desire to lead us in the celebratory dance of that reality.

Finding *Your* Rhythm in God's Joy

1. Psalm 19:1 says, "The heavens are telling of the glory of God; and their expanse is declaring the work of His hands." What are they telling us about God?

When was the last time you went outside at night to
observe and enjoy the stars in the sky and let your
soul fill with awe?

How, specifically, can you incorporate more time in
your schedule to be in nature and let it speak to your
soul?

2. Psalm 16:11 says about God: "In Your right hand there are
   pleasures forever." What brings pleasure to your life?

Do you think that God wants you to experience
pleasure? On what do you base that knowledge?

Are there any ways in which you need to change your opinion about the importance of enjoying life more so that you can "feel" closer to God?

Do you think God created joy for us because he loves us?

3. When Job cried out to God and didn't understand why he was suffering so much, God answered by telling him about the beginning of creation when the angels shouted for joy. What was God trying to say to Job?

4. In what ways does your work and life separate you from nature?

If Romans 1 tells us that "what God made" gives evidence to his existence, then how important is it to our lives to be sure we place ourselves in the midst of nature, to feel and to know his reality?

Dear God, the Artist and Creator of all that is beautiful in the universe,

Thank you for making creation so beautiful. Please open my eyes and my heart to observe the lessons you would teach me about yourself through nature. Let me be like a child and look with delight at the design, beauty, and elements of nature. Thank you for making my world a place where you intended me to experience pleasure, delight, fun, and deep satisfaction. Help me to understand that apart from finding you as the source of that satisfaction, I will not truly experience lasting joy. Help me to order my life so that I may better experience peace and comfort from being in your creation, amidst the beauty you prepared for me to enjoy.

Six

Staying in Step
with Your Partner

Wednesday morning found me brooding over a cup of coffee, alone in the common room of a boarding house in New York City. I felt as if a dark cloud had fallen over me. I was sitting with my Bible open on my lap but not paying attention to it. *Why does everything that we do have to be the hard way?* I thought. *Is my life always going to require bone-tiring work and heartrending struggle just to get through?*

My husband, Clay, and I had traveled to the city to settle our son Nathan into his apartment with his roommates and get him a good start in his first week at the New York Film Academy, where he had received a partial scholarship. Then we planned to spend a much-needed week of vacation celebrating our twenty-fifth wedding anniversary—two years late! Life had been so demanding—what with four children still living at home (three college aged), demanding work deadlines, bills, a move into another home, still trying to parent our thirteen-year-old daughter well, along with feeding everyone (they all expected to eat!), clothing them in relatively clean clothes, purchasing computers for their school and work needs, keeping the cars maintained—that Clay and I just hadn't had the money or time to celebrate our quarter-century mark during the year it occurred.

So this was going to be the week. Clay had arranged for our rooms, had bought tickets to two Broadway plays, and had made dinner reservations at some nice restaurants. We were going to catch our breath from our busy schedules and enjoy each other—like real adults! Taking time to celebrate and remember all that had passed through twenty-five years of marriage was significant to me. We had scheduled eight days there: three to get Nathan settled and five days just to be free and enjoy. The anticipation of that vacation was the anchor and hope that had kept me going through a very busy and demanding summer filled with endless work and projects. No matter what was happening in my life, I always had my trip to New York to look forward to.

But now four days into the trip, things did not look promising. We had arrived at Nate's apartment to discover a big problem. His other roommates had moved in earlier and taken over the three bedrooms that each had a closet and an overhead light. His "bedroom" was really a porch, with French doors and two walls of windows—one looking to the outside and one looking into the living room. No closet, no overhead light, no electric outlets. The French doors opened into his room, limiting where we could place the small mattress. To make matters worse, the room was six by six, and Nate is six feet three. He couldn't even lie down without having to scrunch up his legs.

"You can put your desk in the living room and hang your clothes on a rack by the kitchen," his new roommate said helpfully. Clay and I just looked at each other. We both knew there was *no way* this was going to work! So back to the hotel we went to start again at the drawing board! Of course, having never been to New York City before, we had booked a hotel twelve miles away from his school and were on foot. We had no idea what we were going to do, and we were tired just from moving all of his stuff to our hotel room!

We ate dinner at a café and talked with Nathan about the situation.

He agreed that living there would not give him a good start. He would have no privacy, nowhere to sleep or put his books, computer, desk, or guitar—and he'd still have to pay the same rent as his roommates. So we decided to tackle the problem after a good night of sleep.

The next morning, we identified our top objectives: finding new roommates and a decent place to live. We rode the subway downtown to his school and explained the situation. The office staff gave us their list of students who needed roommates and a few places that had offered student housing. The dorm option was $1,600 a month, not including meals—just housing in a small, shared room. Since this was way beyond Nate's budget, we began to search for apartments. Clay, Nate, and I got to work on our computers and cell phones, following up every lead. The next two days took us to a series of dead ends. Of course, floating around in my mind was the thought that I had been praying all summer for the Lord to provide Nathan with Christian roommates, which added to the profoundness of our problem—since we didn't know a single person in New York!

We rode the subway all over the greater New York City area. We walked literally miles and miles each day, map in hand, cell phones available for calls, and spending all of our adrenaline by midafternoon each day. At night we fell into bed exhausted. We tramped over every possible kind of neighborhood, mostly in areas that looked like ghettos, with barred windows and graffiti over walls and windows (apartments in his price range!). Most of those were at least forty-five minutes by subway to his school. Knowing my son, I was certain that commuting one and a half hours every day, changing trains and subways, would portend badly for him to flourish in this new setting.

As we talked to a variety of people, we were told that New York City had less than 1 percent availability for housing. We also found that most housing agencies charged a big percentage as a finder's fee. So that option was out. After people heard Nate's housing budget ($500), they usually commented, "You'll never be able to find anything below $1,500 a month per person just for a room. And most apartments have rooms with no closet, windows, or lights. On your budget, you'll be fortunate just to get a place to lie on the floor." (Not a reassuring comment for a concerned mom!)

By Tuesday evening, after coming to the end of our list of possibilities, Clay told me in private that he was beginning to wonder if we were going to have to take Nathan back home to Colorado and try to arrange something better for him for the spring semester. At that point, I realized that I hadn't really enlisted prayer support from friends at home. I decided to put out an SOS on my blog about our situation and send e-mails to friends telling them of our dilemma.

> Often in the past, Lord, I have come to thee with a heavy heart and burdened life. And thou hast answered my prayers and graciously lifted the burden from me. Yet with strange perversion, I still refuse to leave my burdens with thee. Always I gather them up—those heavy bundles of fears and anxieties—and shoulder them again.
>
> PETER MARSHALL

WISDOM FROM A "SUPERMAN"

And so it was that I found myself weary, pondering alternatives, and wondering again if all of life was going to be this way! Could *nothing* ever work out smoothly and easily? A myriad of thoughts flurried about in my mind as I read my Bible and prayed that morning. *Satan tempted*

Adam and Eve to disbelieve in God's goodness and provision when they were in the garden, my inner voice told me. *Perhaps he is tempting you to believe that God is not concerned about this! What would it look like for you to live by faith and believe that God is a good Father and that he is going to work in a very personal way for you? What would your requests be if you were convinced he is really listening to your heart and could do what you asked him to do? Can you really live under this dark cloud and have faith and joy in him at the same time? What do you need to do to get out of this discouraged place?*

Then the thought occurred to me, *What would you really want to ask God for if you could? Even if it seems impossible—what are the desires of your heart?*

I took this as the still, small voice of the Holy Spirit. Three specific thoughts immediately came to me. The first was that I really wanted Nathan to live with Christian young men; I wanted him to have fellowship with like-minded believers who could help him ford the very secular cultural stream into which he was stepping. I remembered again that this is what I had been praying for all summer. Second, I really wanted him to be in Manhattan so that he would be close to his school and to the many activities that he would have to attend. Third, I wanted to see him be able to find an apartment for $500 because I knew that was all his loan would cover and we didn't have the money to fund him. Anything more would put extra pressure on him and on us.

As I wrote all of these requests in my journal, I knew how impossible they seemed because everyone had *told* us exactly that! So I made a resolution: *I am going to enjoy this day! The Lord is with me. I am going to believe in your goodness, Lord. Satan would want me to doubt you. I choose to turn my heart away from doubt and stand firmly in your light, expecting you to show me your plan!*

I had a mental picture of being at a fork in the road: one pathway led in the direction of fear, turmoil, and all sorts of ruts in the road; the other pathway pointed to faith. The pathway of faith was good and straight-forward; I knew it would lead me in the direction of a peaceful heart. As I made my resolution, I remembered the biblical promise that the fruit of the Spirit is joy and peace.

With my newfound strength, I felt an almost palpable dispersing of the dark cloud that had weighed so heavily on me, pushing me in the direction of fear and dread. No matter what the end of this story would be, I knew that God was good. But I also knew that I had to choose to turn my mind and heart in the direction of faith in him, and that he would cause all things to work out for the good (Romans 8:28). I closed my Bible and went to see if Clay and Nate were ready to go at it again.

Walking into our bedroom where Nathan was looking at his computer, I said, "I really believe that we are going to find something today, Nate. At least we will try!"

My six-feet-three, blond-haired, blue-eyed son looked up at me and said, "Mom, we have been praying about my moving here for six months. And for two years we've asked God to open doors for me here. *Of course* I believe that God is going to provide. Why would you doubt that?"

As I looked at him I saw him once again as my little six-year-old who had informed me so confidently that God wanted him to grow up to be a superman and save the world. How I loved that little boy heart with its strength of conviction! While the body had grown into manhood, the heart still had the innocence and confidence of a child.

Nate wasn't worried because he knew that God *could* be trusted and that God *would* take good care of him.

God's Work Behind the Scenes

There are times in my life when I pray and pray and wonder if God has heard me because he provides no answer in the way that I can perceive it. Then there are other times when God seems to part the Red Sea. These "seeming miracles" give me hope that he must have heard all of my other prayers that appear yet unanswered. I just have to keep praying and keep waiting until I see his answer and understand what he is doing. But in this particular instance, I really saw the Lord part our Red Sea, which was exactly the reassurance I needed before leaving my nineteen-year-old son in New York City.

After Nathan proclaimed his faith, we prayed together. And within five minutes of that prayer, Nate received a text message from a girl we had just met through the Internet in the midst of our search. Her text said simply, "Check this out," with a Web address and listing attached.

He typed in the address, which connected him to a bulletin board announcement: "Two Christian roommates looking for a third to share an apartment in upper Manhattan." We called immediately, and the young man on the other end told Nathan that he could look online to see the apartment they were hoping to rent. However, a board comprised of a number of the building's residents would have to meet with the boys for an interview to approve them for living there. "I think we should meet before you decide, though," he cautioned, "because my roommate and I have some requirements that we hope our third roommate will be willing to commit to. Can you meet me this afternoon at three o'clock in Central Park near my school?" Of course the answer from Nate was, "Yes!"

In the meantime, we went to the realty Web site, where the potential roommate had said we'd find photos of the apartment. They revealed three newly painted bedrooms, all of which had windows, overhead lights, and privacy. The apartment also had a nice kitchen and a tile entrance. And the rent would be $500 a month for each roommate; just the price we had been praying for!

About forty-five minutes after Nate left to meet this young man, our cell phone rang. His excited voice greeted me. "This sounds too good to be true! The two guys are strong Christians who want a third committed Christian. They have been praying about this for the past couple of weeks. They'd like to have an apartment with like-minded guys who are committed to biblical morality and accountability to Christian ideals. And you'll never guess what else!" Nate explained that the young man he'd just met had spent the summer at the same Christian performing arts festival as Joel, Nathan's older brother. "He knows of Joel and all the leaders that Joel knows! Isn't that amazing? Out of all the people I could find in New York City, God would connect me to a couple of great believers who have my values and even know someone in our family."

Well, we thought this was quite a miracle. But God had even more up his sleeve. First, however, we had to go on foot to find places that would deliver furniture to his new unfurnished apartment. We spent almost six hours in a warehouse to find inexpensive furniture, a few dishes, bedside table, and other assorted items Nate would need. We had to purchase it that day in order to have it delivered before we returned home. So we had to pay for the delivery *before* we knew if the residents' board would accept the boys! We had to pray and make the decision by faith—otherwise what were we going to do with a truckload of furniture, to be delivered the next day to an apartment that had yet to be approved that evening for the boys?

Nine o'clock the next morning found us traipsing in a new neighborhood seeking out Nate's potential new home. If everything came together, my first three desires would be met: Nate would be in Manhattan with Christian roommates for $500 a month. As we walked up to the building, I realized that my fourth unspoken prayer was before me—that it be an attractive building, appeal as a haven, and be a good place to come home to every night.

It was an old, classy building with pots of flowers at the door, which sat across the street from a beautiful park! His new roommate was wait-ing for us at the door. "We had no problem getting accepted at the hear-ing last night, so everything is all set!" he informed us.

We walked up the stairs to the fifth floor. Everything was light and clean and fresh—just what I would have hoped. I couldn't have imagined two days before that such a change would take place in Nate's situation. Within five minutes the truck arrived with his stuff. Settling it all in took several hours and multiple trips. We hauled suitcases, groceries, and boxes up all five flights of stairs. Finally, it looked as if we had helped as much as we could.

I was like a giddy little girl thinking that I was actually going to be alone with Clay and *finally* celebrate our anniversary! We would see *Mary Poppins* on Broadway and live as adults, even if it was just for two days! Having Nate's rollaway cot removed from the foot of our bed even made our hotel room seem more luxurious. We were so exhausted from our week of tromping all over New York City, though, that we fell soundly asleep within seconds of our heads hitting the pillows! The next day was a blur of having tea, street shopping, and eating an unhurried adult dinner.

Sunday morning found us lingering in our bed to catch up on sleep. As I lay there, I reflected that this week had definitely not been what I'd thought it would be. I had not celebrated leisurely romantic days with my sweetheart, dining, getting much-needed rest, and reviewing our ideals for the years ahead. Instead, we had run constantly, worried, stressed, and kept Nathan in our hotel room instead of having our own room. But we had also spent time on our knees seeking God for a miracle! And that's what we got.

Later that morning, Clay and I met Nate at a traditional New York cupcake bakery. I looked forward to hearing how Nate was faring in his new home and wondered how it had gone with his new roommates.

As Nate devoured his cupcake and milk, he remembered something. "Guess what? You won't believe the story of my other roommate." Then he told us that the young man had grown up in the same Texas town as some of our dear friends and knew them well. "He went to school in Boston before he moved here to try to work on Broadway."

My interest was piqued. One of my friends had a son who had moved to Boston to attend a conservatory and was hoping to move to New York.

"Maybe your roommate knows of my friend's son since they're from the same town and both attended a music conservatory in Boston." When I told him the young man's name, Nate stared back at me, mouth agape.

"Mom, that's his name. He's the other guy I'm rooming with!"

I could hardly believe it! Nathan was going to room with a young man I had known for ten years! I had stayed in his home and had breakfast with him when he was a teen. His mom had invited me to speak to her women's group ten years before, and we had become friends over the years. I'd even had her speak at one of my women's conferences. She would e-mail me from time to time with prayer requests for her two boys, but I thought her son was still in Boston. And to think that the young man I had been praying for was going to live with Nathan!

Just then my cell phone rang.

"Sally!" my friend said excitedly. "Can you believe it? Our boys are going to live together. It's like finding a needle in a haystack. We've been praying for a third Christian roommate with the same values! I never could have imagined it would be Nate."

We were all stunned. To think that out of the millions of people in New York City and the endless apartments to sift through, the Lord had very specifically answered all of our prayers by sending our boys, providentially, over the Internet, to find each other. And now, these young men—one who had been with my older son all summer and the other, the son of a trusted and beloved friend of mine—would be in New York City together.

I pictured heaven's operators receiving all these prayer requests from different people all over the United States—some my friends and some her friends. All of us had been asking God to direct our boys to a suitable, inexpensive apartment to share with strong Christians. Then God became a heavenly prayer coordinator putting these requests together and coming up with a suitable miracle that would satisfy and please all of us!

The Lord worked in such a personal way to let me know that he was gong to take care of my son's needs, even in New York City! I knew he must have a plan for Nathan if he went to all that trouble to so amazingly answer our heartfelt prayers.

> The fruit of the Spirit is love, joy, peace, patience,
> kindness, goodness, faithfulness, gentleness,
> self-control; against such things there is no law.
>
> GALATIANS 5:22–23

HOW TO SOOTHE A TROUBLED HEART

I pondered the whole process as Clay and I flew back to Colorado—especially what it revealed about so much of our lives. Certainly, many of our days are filled with stress and seemingly unanswered prayers. We face so many difficulties as a regular part of everyday living. Not the life-challenging difficulties such as cancer or death or divorce, but rather the wearying, daily drainers such as conflict in the home, a demanding boss, loneliness amidst a busy life, a traffic ticket, a leaky washing machine, a child with chronic ear infections or asthma, an unexpected bill, a busy schedule, and a computer that always crashes during a deadline.

Jesus said, "In the world you have tribulation" (John 16:33).

I will have trouble, stress, pressure. That should be a no-brainer to me. So why did I continue to be surprised when tribulation came upon me? The weariness would set in. I would dread what a day might hold, wondering what else would or could be difficult. I know this sounds like a whiny little girl—but that is how I felt sometimes. I was tired of the burdens and the stress.

But in viewing the recent experience as part of my quest to understand joy, I realized a new facet of how to keep my heart joyful and manage the stress so that it doesn't affect the mood and moments of my day. Paul writes in Galatians 5:22 that "the fruit of the Spirit is…joy." So if the Holy Spirit resides in me as a child of God, then the fruit of his Spirit—including joy—is already a part of my heart. It is not something I have to conjure; it is already there.

What happens when I don't feel joyful? A verse farther down in Galatians hints at the answer: "If we live by the Spirit, let us also walk by the Spirit" (verse 25). So I am to walk by the Holy Spirit day by day, moment by moment. I am to walk next to him, walk with him, walk in his presence, let his presence give me the joy that comes from him residing in me. I am to live by the power of the Holy Spirit.

I happened to be reading in the gospel of John shortly after I returned from my trip to New York, and I noticed something else that helped to clarify this concept for me. Three times John mentioned that Jesus himself was troubled in his heart. In John 11:33, when Jesus saw Mary weeping after the death of her brother, Lazarus, he was "deeply moved in spirit and was troubled." John 12:27 records that in response to his feelings about dying for our salvation, Jesus said, "Now My soul has become troubled." And finally, in John 13:21, Jesus "became troubled in spirit," pondering that one of his disciples was going to betray him.

All of these passages show that in his humanity, Jesus was troubled. These incidents were certainly very serious and would bring great anguish to *anyone's* soul. But it spoke to my heart to understand that Jesus himself felt the stress of living in this fallen world. If Jesus became troubled and he was perfect, then being troubled might be a normal part of my experience as well. And I also found it reassuring that he knew how to break free.

In John 14:1, Jesus addressed what we are to do when we are troubled. In talking with his disciples in the upper room on the night before he was crucified, Jesus said, "Do not let your heart be troubled." In other words, in our heart—where our emotions and commitments and all that we hold dear is held—we are not to allow ourselves to be troubled. This tells me that there is a solution for when we feel troubled. It tells me that I have the ability to keep my heart from being troubled. Jesus followed with the simple answer, "Believe in God, believe also in Me."

That does not mean that the difficulties go away but that our heart doesn't have to *stay* troubled or depressed. The key is, when our heart is troubled we need to believe in God. Maintaining a moment by moment walk in the power of the Holy Spirit means that we continually practice trusting in God, believing in his reality, living in the confidence that he will work all things together for our good.

Belief is the antidote for a troubled heart: believing in God, believing that he is with us, believing that he is good, believing that he can take care of our trouble, believing in his presence with us every minute, and not looking to the limitations of our circumstances! In studying these concepts, I have realized that often the difference between two people who both are in difficult circumstances is that one believes in God's presence and provision in the midst of her circumstances, while the other has allowed the intensity of the situation to determine the state of her heart.

Jesus' antidote to keeping our hearts from being troubled is belief, or faith. Hebrews 11:1 tells us that faith (or belief in God) is "the assurance of things hoped for, the conviction of things not seen." Believing in the invisible Christ and calling upon that belief in every situation—*that* is faith.

Walking in joy, by the resources of the Holy Spirit who abides in me, is simply believing in him, turning our eyes to him, leaning on him. Simple faith. But I must be vigilant to *remain* in this place of joy. I must stop the troublesome thoughts and feelings the moment they begin to invade my heart and turn immediately to him, choosing to believe in his presence and goodness.

PRACTICING "JOY CHECKS"

A friend shared with me her solution for keeping on track with God. "I have learned to do 'joy checks' in regards to my spirit," she explained. "I have noticed that often when I go through my days, suddenly I'll realize I have a bad attitude or I'm feeling anxious or stressed or irritated. If I discipline myself, I can almost always trace back my thought or actions to see just where I got off the path with the Lord."

She explained her insight in more detail: "Often, it is an irritation at a person or a difficult circumstance that has taken me in the wrong direction and has fostered within me a wrong attitude. Sometimes, it is a strong fear or reaction to something that is required of me. It can be a myriad of things. But since I have learned the habit of immediately checking why I am feeling off balance, I can almost always put my finger on what I need to do to get back in step. It always requires dealing with an attitude, feeling, insecurity, or anger. If I don't deal with the sin or wrong attitude, I continue down the road to destructive feelings. But the sooner I deal with the root of my feelings, the easier it is to get back in step with the Lord."

This joy check made sense to me. I could see that perhaps my own joy has stopped at the point in which I begin to lead and attempt to drag God in the direction I feel is most beneficial. Yet if I am to follow his lead in my dance of life, I must lean into him and respond to his direction. I must remember that the Spirit has already provided me with joy as a result of dwelling within me. Then as an act of my will, I must choose to put my belief in him, that he will take care of me and all the details of my life.

Yesterday, I was on a mission to get my work finished. I drove downtown toward a quiet hotel where I would be free to write without any interruptions. I had to stop on the way because my gas tank was on empty. (Someone had borrowed my car and left it without gas!) Next, I stopped at a coffee shop. Before I ordered, I saw a mug on sale and thought, *I would much rather drink out of a real mug,* so I bought it. I turned to walk away from the counter—and promptly dropped my new purchase. It shattered into hundreds of pieces. I bent down to clean it up and saw that the coffee had spilled on my new shirt. Finally after I cleaned up the mess and fixed my shirt as best as I could, I got on the road again—and was promptly halted by a long, unexpected construction detour.

Tempted to become irritated at how my day was going, I decided to give this book and its deadline over to the Lord. I would choose not to pay attention to the broken mug and my dirty shirt; it's just part of normal life. So I put on some quiet instrumental music, sat back in my seat, and enjoyed the peace as I waited to move through the congested traffic.

A commitment to living a life of joy involves a one-time decision in our heart: "Lord, I want to know your joy every day of my life, and I will seek to find out what it means to dwell in your presence in joy."

Experiencing joy, though, is a long-term process—a journey toward maturity as we begin to be aware of those thoughts and worries that would steal our joy. The more we practice taking all of our troubled thoughts captive, the more easily we will recognize them before they take hold in our heart. Practice and discipline provide strength training for our mental muscles and heart responses. So walking in the reality of joy is a road we truly find only as we mature and become stronger. The more consistently we follow that path—believing in God's goodness and turning away from Satan's taunts—the more the habit to submit to the Lord and trust him becomes second nature.

We can make a commitment to take every situation, every feeling, every fear to God as it happens. We don't have to remain in a state of emotional separation from the Lord every time we get out of step. We simply have to practice walking each step with him and allow his presence to bring us the joy that comes from resting in the arms of our capable dance partner through each measure of life's song.

Finding *Your* Rhythm in God's Joy

1. Paul wrote, "We are destroying speculations and every lofty thing raised up against the knowledge of God, and we are taking every thought captive to the obedience of Christ" (2 Corinthians 10:5). What does it mean to take every thought in your head "captive" to the obedience of Christ?

Are there any specific patterns of thought (fear, jealousy, irritation, impatience) that you struggle with? How does this rob your joy?

What do you need to do to change that pattern?

2. We know that for Christians the fruit of the Spirit is joy (Galatians 5:22). If you are a believer, and the Holy Spirit resides in you, what role does he play in producing the fruit of joy in your life?

Is God at work to help you?

How can you learn to hear more of his voice of encouragement and wisdom throughout your day?

3. Jesus said, "Do not let your heart be troubled; believe in God, believe also in Me" (John 14:1). What regularly troubles your heart?

What do you need to believe about God in order to move from being troubled to having his joy?

4. What would it take for you to begin practicing "joy checks"? Practice recognizing all the thoughts and feelings that lead you away from trusting God. Then choose to turn the eyes of your heart upon his goodness and trust in him.

Dear heavenly Father,

I want to be mature in my faith. Help me not to give attention to the trivial and troubling issues of my life. Please help me to honor you in my mind, by choosing to believe in your goodness and love for me, even in the midst of my stress. Teach me how to abide in your Spirit and how to walk with you so that I may experience your joy each moment of my day. In Jesus' name I come. Amen.

Seven

Joy Is Made Full
When It's Shared

As I began the journey of writing this book, I made a list of impressions and memories about my experiences of joy. By far the most common link among these pleasurable moments is that I had enjoyed them with someone who loved me.

It makes sense that joy is connected to relationship because it was of such great value to Jesus. He said that the two most important commandments, which summed up all the Law and the prophets, were to love God and to love people (see Matthew 22:37–40). The only one-word definition of God in the Bible is "God is *love*" (1 John 4:16). Paul tells us in 1 Corinthians 13 that even if we give our money to the poor and can speak amazingly well and do all sorts of miracles but we do not have love, we are "a noisy gong or clanging symbol" (verse 1).

Friendships and family relationships can be the places we most feel God's love as we experience it at the hands of human beings. As I pondered the connection in my own life between a joyful heart and relationship with people, one particular person came to mind. This friend became the starting point for me to learn the joy that comes from committed, unconditional love. She provided a model of committed love, which I was able to carry over in to my marriage, parenting, and ministry.

It all began on a dark, misty winter night in Vienna, Austria. Since it was February 1, my mom's birthday, I have always remembered the date. How could I have known that this particular evening, in the midst of the hustle and bustle of catching a tram, crowding in amongst strangers, and standing outside in the below-zero, frigid cold would be so momentous? This was the evening I would begin my Jonathan–David relationship with the woman who would become like a sister to me.

Having moved there six months earlier, I was the Austrian "expert" of the two of us, and so I planned the tramway stop, a midway point on the city map between our two apartments, as our meeting place. Wanting to seem confident, I eyed what I thought was a little local café across the street, an adequate location for our first conversation.

Previously, I had lived in Texas with a girl who had once been the roommate of this girl I was about to meet. When my friend found out I was going to meet her old roommate, she said, "I can't imagine anyone more different from you than Gwennie. You have almost nothing in common. She's an easygoing, Kentucky girl who's been living in conservative Massachusetts, and you're a passionate, extroverted Texas girl working with 'rah, rah' sorority girls on a large campus. I can't even imagine how you're going to get along as partners in Eastern Europe. Good luck!"

With her words still fresh in my mind, my expectations for sharing a friendship with this new acquaintance were not too high. But we were the first two women who had volunteered to work in Communist Poland for Campus Crusade for Christ, and so as unlikely a set of partners as we seemed, we were all each other had for a ministry team.

I waited in the chilly fog for a tall, blond, twenty-six-year-old American girl to exit from the tram. Each time a tram stopped, my heart would race as my eyes scanned the crowds of people scrambling on and off the car. Finally, I spotted a young woman who seemed likely to be her. Her friendly demeanor and taupe jacket shouted "American" in a sea of dark coats, as she stepped down from the back of the tram, looking insecurely around the crowd of noisy, young teens who had exited at the same stop. I waved at her. With a look of relief, she began to walk toward me.

I guided us toward the café across the street, which I hoped would be a warm haven. We stepped through the door—and found ourselves in a smoke-filled, pungent nook, the only women in a room full of loud, bawdy men. It was not a café as I'd expected; it was a bar. This was not a place where one would expect a positive, life-changing meeting to occur. But it became a sanctuary of camaraderie for two young American girls about to begin the momentous adventure of missions in a Communist country. In this place God began to knit together two souls of true kindred spirits, marked by a passionate desire to bring the love of Christ to a nation that had experienced repression and governmental restrictions for evangelical outreach.

We talked easily about everything in the world for almost two hours before I even checked my watch. It wasn't just me directing the conversation; Gwen took time to find out about me and to ask penetrating questions that took us below the surface issues of our lives. Stimulating conversation flowed between us as we shared personal stories about how the Lord had brought us from America all the way to this foreign place with a dream of bringing God's light and forgiveness to a Communist country whose gates were tightly shut to Christians. The external trappings of our differing personalities and cultural background faded in light of the stirring passion we both felt for this cause that bound our hearts together.

I think God must have been smiling at the treasure he had planned to give to me and my soon-to-be lifelong best friend. The connection between us wasn't only because of our need to have each other as a support system; it was about our deep sense of shared spirituality. There is a palpable energy and life to relationships forged on ideals, faith, and hope. Friendship forged in the work of God's kingdom is the best kind. The grandness of the calling supersedes the small, selfish issues that abound in relationships and gives us a grace to accept each other as we are.

In Jesus' life, even the hearts of the disciples were intimately and forever knit together because of the countless moments of living, laughing, learning, and engaging in life with Christ. His call to them was to become fishers of men—to step out of ordinary life and become part of the eternal work of his kingdom. Even as this group of young, idealistic "Jesus followers" rallied to become a part of a calling much bigger than themselves, so their hearts were galvanized because of their common purpose of making him known. The gold of such fires was also kindled in our own hearts that night, and Gwen and I found ourselves part of the great historic call, which had provided the ground in which so many other great friendships had been planted through the centuries.

We began to take trips together on rough, bumpy trains and speeding taxis into cities and towns where we met with strangers who were awaiting our arrival. Often the beds would be hard, the food sparse and strange. But teaching the Word of God to those who longed for such teaching satisfied our souls. Over a period of time, we took on roles with each other. Gwen was often the provider, bringing food to give us refreshment between the meals on our long trips—a hot thermos of coffee, boiled eggs, cheese and ham sandwiches on crisp semmels (the star-shaped kaiser rolls so common in all Austrian bakeries). And of course we could not have lived without her "gorp": peanuts, raisins, and chocolate chips or M&M's. Gorp became a mainstay as we traveled in trains and taxis over literally thousands of miles.

I played the part of ministry leader, doing much of the teaching, arranging the meetings, setting up appointments with people, leading the Bible studies, and helping with train schedules. Other times Gwen would do the teaching and I would handle the "provider" role. We became true partners in the sense of filling in the cracks of what needed to be done. We both served and carried our weight in a spirit of grace, loving and giving in a mutually blessed relationship.

Eventually, Gwen and I moved into a tiny fourth-floor apartment in Krakow, Poland. Wanting greater personal access to people, we took the risk of moving into Communist Poland from the politically free country of Austria, hoping it would open more doors for ministry. We had to walk up four flights of stairs with our books, luggage, and groceries, and yet our warm rooms seemed a heavenly refuge. We even had a secret room hidden behind a wall of bookshelves. Putting pressure in the right place on this panel of shelves would hit a spring door and open the wall into a tiny room. Our hideout was furnished, almost wall-to-wall, with two long, thin beds that would allow for missionary visitors to stay with us, hidden away, without bringing suspicion to others who might come unexpectedly to our apartment.

Friendship doubles our joy and divides our grief.

Swedish proverb

A Friendship Forged Through Challenges

Attending the Jagiellonian University as students, while studying the Polish language, was our cover for getting a visa to stay in the country. Times were tough, as we didn't have much nutritious food and we lived an isolated, sometimes lonely existence. The Polish language was strange and difficult for us to learn. We had few support systems, and we lived constantly under the threat of being discovered as undercover missionaries.

About midnight one night, two soldiers began banging on our door, calling our names in Polish and demanding that we allow them to enter. They continued banging and shouting loudly for several hours. We kept our door bolted and prayed desperately that the soldiers would leave. Every resident in the building must have heard the noise, but because everyone feared the secret police or any official, no one came out of their apartments to check on us. All night we huddled together and whispered prayers for God's protection, with our knees literally knocking from fear. I wouldn't have lasted in this Communist country but for my friend Gwennie being God's hands and words, comfort and encouragement to give me courage to stay and invest my life in real people.

Routine helped bring joy and beauty into our otherwise challenging lives. Every afternoon after class, we took a walk around the city park together or strolled along the Vistula River, sometimes as much as five to seven miles at a time. Having a friend to talk with and to share moments with gave both of us a small sense of community and kept us healthy. Each evening at dinner (even if it was one more night of eggs, since vegetables and meat were difficult to come by!), we would light little candles, put on beautiful music, and read stories aloud to each other. Those things brought entertainment and enjoyment. These were the glorious days before television and cable had become much of an option for entertainment. *Treasures of the Snow,* a children's book written by Patricia St. John, was one of the delightful tales I will always remember us reading together.

Gwen often left me encouraging notes, brought flowers to cheer me, and served me in practical ways, such as by cleaning our apartment, organizing our papers, or doing other tedious tasks.

Once we took a trip to London as a sort of break from the grind. Between the two of us, we had about $700 American money to spend over the two weeks we would be gone. Soon after we arrived at a friend's apartment, Gwen discovered that she needed emergency dental care. The bill totaled almost $700. We both had to chip in all of our money just to pay her bill. Very little was left for food or treats on our holiday away.

Toward the end of our trip, Gwen insisted that we celebrate my birthday, even though we didn't have much money left. She said she wanted to take me to tea. While we were sitting at the table chitchatting, a quiet alarm on a handheld calculator started to beep. Gwen clapped her hands together and excitedly pronounced, "That means it's present time!" She pulled out a lovely little wrapped package from her shoulder bag and gave it to me. "Happy birthday, Sally!" This happened three more times during our tea, and soon everyone around us was waiting to see what the alarm would produce for my birthday.

"How did you manage this with our limited funds?" I asked, perplexed.

"Oh, I've been planning this for a long time. I wrapped all the presents in Poland and brought them with me." She had planned celebration and happiness for me way ahead of my birthday. As I looked at this sweet friend, I realized anew that she was a picture of God's humor, devoted love, and friendship. It was as though he was letting me see that if he provided such a friend to help me make it as a missionary, he must love me very dearly.

What fun I have even today as I think about that crazy alarm going off. She has even done the alarm for my children in restaurants, giving them hysterical joy in the midst of mundane moments. Laughter and fun is an instrumental part of God's personality—and he taught me about those character traits through my friend.

A COVENANT FRIENDSHIP

While Gwen and I were in Poland, we did a Bible study on David and Jonathan, who, as Saul's son, was in line to be the future king until God chose David instead. The two committed to being covenant friends for the rest of their lives. It meant they would always be loyal, always be like family to each other, take care of each other's family, and be willing even to die for each other. Gwennie and I decided that God wanted us to be covenant friends as well. So we prayed and committed our relationship to the Lord.

Little did we know how far he would take us in our decision. While I eventually moved back to America, got married, and had children, Gwennie stayed in Vienna for twenty-four years. She then moved back to Kentucky to take care of her eighty-seven-year-old mother, who had increasing needs.

During her many years in missions, her father, both of her brothers, and two close aunts who were like grandmothers to her died. Each time someone passed away, God worked it so that Gwen was with me—even though we rarely lived in the same city. It was as though God wanted her to be personally comforted through me, his representative of love to her. In addition, with so many deaths in Gwen's life and her infirm mom the only surviving close relative, she needed a family to give her community and meaning. We've had the privilege of serving as that family. Just last week, my twenty-four-year-old daughter, Sarah, who has become like a daughter to Gwen, was visiting with her when Gwen's mother suffered a stroke and had to be taken to the hospital in an ambulance. Again, instead of Gwen being alone, this family relationship kept Gwen from feeling alone or unsupported during this crisis.

God also had a plan in mind for Gwen to meet my needs in ways we could never have anticipated when we first committed to covenant friendship. How could I have known that Clay and I would become emotionally separated from our extended family because of certain difficulties? This meant that we would almost always be without any family on holidays, birthdays, or any celebration days. Yet I believe that the

Lord knew we would feel like orphans and so sent Gwennie to be a joy to us—to be family and to care for us deeply. She has made us feel that God had not abandoned us but understands our need for committed family. Every Christmas season for twenty-seven years, Gwen made the long trip to our home and came with a trunk filled with little gifts and trinkets for me, my husband, and four children. Because of her commitment to make the expensive trip, my children grew up thinking of her as family. She never missed a birthday, always taking delight in reaching out to my children.

Because our friendship has been built on commitment, we have disciplined ourselves to make each other a priority. Though sometimes I travel twenty weekends a year speaking and keep busy in my writing career, not to mention my involvement in the lives of my husband and four children and handling everything that goes into keeping a home balanced and centered, I put my responsibility to Gwen right up at the top. I commit to visiting her one or two times a year. I make time for phone calls to her even though I am allergic to the phone! We pray over the phone. We e-mail. We stay connected in each other's lives.

Just as the Father has loved Me, I have also loved you; abide in My love. If you keep My commandments, you will abide in My love; just as I have kept My Father's commandments and abide in His love. These things I have spoken to you so that My joy may be in you, and that your joy may be made full. This is My commandment, that you love one another, just as I have loved you. Greater love has no one than this, that one lay down his life for his friends.

JOHN 15:9-13

LIFE-LAYING-DOWN KIND OF LOVE

As I think about the connection between joy and friendship, I think about Jesus' words on the subject in John 15:9–13:

> Just as the Father has loved Me, I have also loved you; abide in
> My love. If you keep My commandments, you will abide in My
> love; just as I have kept My Father's commandments and abide in
> His love. These things I have spoken to you so that My joy may
> be in you, and that your joy may be made full. This is My com-
> mandment, that you love one another, just as I have loved you.
> Greater love has no one than this, that one lay down his life for
> his friends.

I find it curious that Jesus said, "These things I have spoken to you so that My joy may be in you, and that your joy may be made full." He wanted his disciples to be joyful—full of joy! And he was telling them how. He gave them a whole list of connections, and it is all about rela-tionship! He said that we are to obey him and that if we do, we will abide in his love, live there, dwell there, flourish there in his love. And then he went on to define the commandment that will help us to abide in his love and experience full joy: "This is My commandment, that you love one another." That's it? Not that we have to be perfect or holy or right-eous or without sin, but that we love one another? That is where our joy is made full?

Absolutely. This is why Jesus commanded us to cultivate and be committed to "life-laying-down," serving, loyal love.

As I consider this passage in light of my most committed "love" rela-tionships—marriage to Clay, who has stuck with me through thick and thin for almost thirty years; Gwen (and a few other close friends), who have loved and accepted me unconditionally for more than thirty years; my children, who are the closest of friends and beloved of my heart—I realize that it has been in my relationships with them that I have had the most joyful memories, the deepest intimate encounters, the greatest celebrations of life. I have felt deeply loved and accepted in the common life experiences that have knit our souls together. And it all came through committed, "I will be loyal to you and love you no matter what" love.

I also see that severed relationships have kept so many of the people I know from having joy. Any broken relationship is like a divorce: it tears a portion of our heart apart when something that was made to be whole is broken. I wonder if a statement opposite of Jesus' could also be true, "You will not experience fully my Father's love, nor have your joy be full, if you refuse to love one another. That is what will keep you from experiencing the intimate love of God and the fullness of joy in life—because you were created for love!" And I also wonder if a statement such as "Greater love will a person lose if he is not willing to lay down his life for his friend" is true as well.

This laying down of our lives—serving, giving, helping—is the key to real friendship and love, and ultimately, the fullness of joy. What does that look like? Looking back at the passage, Jesus said, "Just as the Father has loved Me, I have also loved you." How has he loved us? He gave up his throne in heaven and came to the earth as a simple, humble man. He lived and loved and served and healed and poured out his life and died on the cross to pay for our sins. So that becomes the standard for what he means when he says, "Love one another."

If our relationships are built around serving God and obeying Christ by laying down our lives for others, then our giving love will be about pleasing God—regardless of how the other person responds. Every relationship becomes meaningful in light of doing what God wants us to do—to love—so that our joy can be made full. Therefore, loving is not dependent on the other person's behavior, his immaturity, his inconsistencies, his selfishness, or any other way he might have hurt me. Rather, our love is given as Christ gave his love to us—generously, graciously, and freely.

There is something very freeing about loving in this biblical way. I can always succeed. I can always be at peace no matter how the relationship goes. If I please Christ by laying down my life, then I have done what was expected of me.

THE GIVER OF ISOLATION AND THE THIEF OF JOY

It seems to me that loneliness and isolationism are rampant in our society. People live in different cities and states away from their family members. Divorce—the picture of a lack of love and the refusal to lay down a life—is more prominent than ever before in history. Many of my closest friends have been injured through the breakup of a marriage. Single mothers abound, often having never married—having had a sexual experience to create a child but not the foundational committed love that nurtures a long-term relationship. Children grow up without a sense of connection to a family that is committed to loving them, and consequently, they lack a clear picture of what God's love looks like.

So many have lost a sense of community. It is rare for people to know their neighbors. At many megachurches, congregants drive from miles away, so local relationships are difficult to establish. The largeness of these communities of believers automatically means that thousands can come through the church doors every week while remaining totally unknown by anyone else present.

And let's face it: many relationships with co-workers, neighbors, family, and friends are just plain hard and irritating and can be broken over petty issues. There is great potential for hurt feelings and offense just from knowing sinful people (which includes all of us) whose personalities or values are different from ours. We all experience such difficult relationships.

All of these details add to the breakdown of true friendship and to the difficulty of cultivating love in life-laying-down relationships. We've lost one of the most important sources of the joy God intended us to experience. And so loneliness and emptiness abound.

One of the underlying reasons for this breakdown is that people are looking for deep fulfillment in their empty lives apart from God's design, apart from loving people in the context of loving, serving, and obeying God. Instead they pursue relationships that have no ultimate purpose or divine glue to hold them together. And so it is possible to go from one activity to the other, one sexual experience to another, and never find that hollow place in life filled up.

Humans are created to be God's hands of comfort, God's words of affection and appreciation, God's face of love, and God's works of service and help. We are created to be one of the venues in which the Spirit of God demonstrates the reality of his own unconditional love. Friendships and other close relationships provide opportunities for people to feel the love of God through words and touch, given by real people who are prompted by his Spirit.

True, fulfilling love is based on the principle of laying down your life for your friend. Love that accepts the limitations of each friend, spouse, or child. Love that overcomes petty irritations and differences with the strength of God's gracious love. When marriage, parenting, and friendships follow this servant model of love, intimacy will happen, support systems will be intact, and community will be formed. And then Jesus' promise will be fulfilled: our joy will be full.

Hope for Broken Relationships

God designed relationships to be the basis in which we could experience the joy of knowing his wonderful committed love toward us, as well as the deep love intended to bind our hearts to other humans. But when relationships aren't fortified with God's purposes and wisdom principles for cultivating intimacy, they easily break. This leaves many gazing at a string of broken or shallow relationships, while still longing deep inside to be loved.

Broken relationships exist everywhere. I see it in the lives of many people I counsel, and I experience it in my own life. Yet in Christ, we have hope for redemption, even when relationships have been marred and destroyed. People often want to hold on to bitterness and blame rather than to cultivate the unconditional love and intimacy of the Father. Choosing to love as he loved, by laying aside their differences and grievances, is a foreign concept to many people. The passage in John, however, indicates that loving-each-other relationships are connected not only to our joy being full but also to experiencing the love and intimacy of God our Father.

In a fallen world, we are all exposed to many difficult and harmful relationships. And yet we don't have to carry that baggage on our shoulders. Paul tells us in Romans 12: "So far as it depends on you, be at peace with all men" (verse 18). This means that I am obligated to lay down my life, to be humble, to ask for forgiveness, but when I have done all that I can, I can be free of this burden if I just give it to God, ask him to take care of it, and then live my life in peace.

We cannot make others "act" in love. We cannot make irrational people be rational. We cannot force others to respond to us or to forgive us. They have volition of their own. And so we must leave them to God. We *are* responsible, though, to initiate forgiveness toward others, to be committed to love unconditionally, and to seek out friendship. Only then can we know the intimate love of God and experience true peace and joy.

Jesus was our model on how best to pursue those things. In 1 Peter 2, we read about Jesus' attitude toward others even as he was being crucified: "While being reviled, He did not revile in return...but kept entrusting Himself to Him who judges righteously" (verse 23). In the midst of being rejected as God, Jesus did not retaliate. He gave his life into his Father's hands and died in peace—trusting, even in death, in God's forever love. Even his last thought was of loving and extending grace to his accusers: "Father, forgive them; for they do not know what they are doing" (Luke 23:34).

So this is our mandate: we are called to initiate friendship, love, forgiveness, and trust. It is the way to joy. Dancing with our Father becomes an intimate celebration of extending his love, of identifying with his sacrificial, winsome love that redeemed our lives. We participate in the joyful rhythm of extending his life to others as he has extended his life to us.

Cultivating a "Love" Way of Life

Recently, I planned a visit with Gwennie on my birthday because I knew we would have great fun, and I knew she would spoil me! (Best friends do that for each other.) After she drove two hours to pick me up at the airport, we spent a lovely evening over dinner catching up in her home in Kentucky. Early the next morning we took another two-hour drive to Louisville, in sweltering heat, for a speaking engagement I had. She volunteered to assist me, so we worked all day without a break, with Gwen faithfully helping me sell books and counsel people. Midafternoon, we packed up and decided to stop at a café for a quick bite to eat before hurrying home to take care of her elderly mom.

While lingering over our last bit of lunch, I asked her, "How are you really doing?" (Between the lines I was really asking her, "How are you doing in this sixth year of taking care of your mom twenty-four hours a day while her health deteriorates? Knowing that she isn't really even aware of the sacrifice you have made by giving up your own life in Europe to take care of her basic needs every day.")

Her immediate answer was, "I have a joyful heart."

"What do you mean?"

"I feel like all of us choose whether to look at life from the glass half-full or half-empty perspective. I have made a concerted effort over the years to look at my life in light of all that God has provided for me. I have determined to find joy and to cultivate contentment so that I can have the strength and courage to face every day."

She took a sip of her coffee, then continued. "When I look for joy, I find it everywhere and see God's hand in my life in very intimate ways. I have a sweet cottage all my own. I have developed new friends in my neighborhood. I have fellowship with friends in a Bible study each week. I open my home for many all over my tiny town and am busy caring for them—I have lots of people to love and who give love back to me. I have so much to be joyful about. If I allow my mind to begin going toward dark thoughts, though, it becomes a downward spiral. And I know that a joyful heart will serve me much better and make my life more pleasant."

Not only has Gwen brought me joy, but she has modeled choosing joy. I've learned from her about joy in a more personal way because of our friendship. Immediately, my mind remembered the verse, "A joyful heart is good medicine, but a broken spirit dries up the bones" (Proverbs 17:22). How evident in her life was the result of cultivating and focusing on joy; it was just the medicine she needed. It was just the message God wanted me to hear. And all from the lips of a beloved friend.

This commitment was even reflected in her home, which is an inviting shelter of beauty, wonderful meals, and lots of great discussion. Her lovely cottage, the home in which she grew up, is small and located in a once-thriving older mining community that exhibits only a few remnants of better days. Yet when Gwen left the mission field to take care of her mom, she decided to make the home a retreat for all who would visit. She painted and restored one outdated room at a time, making each into a place of beauty. Planting new flowers, rosebushes, and trees, she restored the yard of her childhood to a place of splendor. In the hours that her mom slept, she studied cookbooks and fixed gourmet meals for all who would come to her home.

Her sweet mother, who was a gentle, loving woman, is now in a phase of life where she has lost all ability to be cognitive of what Gwen is providing for her. She lives much of her life with a blank slate in her mind, pondering from time to time moments of her childhood. Even in the pain of watching her mother "go away," Gwennie has chosen, in light of her sweet childhood memories, to honor her mother and God by relentlessly working to bring life, beauty, love, joy, and warmth to others' lives.

I always know that when I visit Gwen, she will have a Bible verse or an insight to share with me from her daily quiet times with God. She has a reservoir of encouragement to give because of almost forty years of walking with the Lord every day. And through her friendship and love I have benefited so much from God's love.

The difficulties and losses she has had over the years—the whys that will never be answered, lonely nights and weeks, disappointments, the lack of a marriage partner and children, the death of her family members, and so many more questions—are faced with trust in God, love of people, and a heart to serve. This invisible joy in her heart has made her one of the most life-giving, encouraging people I have ever met. Beloved by hundreds of people all over the world, she embodies what Christ said, "If you keep My commandments, you will abide in My love; just as I have kept My Father's commandments and abide in His love. These things I have spoken to you so that My joy may be in you, and that your joy may be made full" (John 15:10–11).

So this is our mandate: to love as he loved us. How? By initiating, loving, forgiving, trusting. Make a list of people to call or meet for coffee. Have a dinner for friends or those who need encouragement twice a month. Volunteer at a children's Sunday school. Start a book discussion club.

In the shared music of relationship, as we swirl in a circle of giving and receiving love, we find ourselves drawn to a joy made complete.

Finding *Your* Rhythm in God's Joy

1. In John 15:12, Jesus said, "This is My commandment, that you love one another, just as I have loved you." How has Jesus loved you? How does that mean you should love others?

   Is there any relationship in your life in which you have not loved the person as Christ has commanded? What can you do to make this relationship right?

2. Peter told us in 1 Peter 2:23 that Jesus, "while being reviled, He did not revile in return…but kept entrusting Himself to Him who judges righteously." If we follow the model of Christ, what should we do when we find ourselves in an "unfair" relationship, in which we are rejected or harshly treated?

    Are there any relationships in which you need to follow his example?

    How can you find joy in those situations?

3. Proverbs 17:22 says, "A joyful heart is good medicine, but a broken spirit dries up the bones." In relationships how can you cultivate a "joyful" heart?

Is there anything that has broken your spirit?

How does loving others and serving them for the sake
of the God who serves and loves you, bring healing to
your whole body and heart?

What steps do you need to take to serve more, give
more, and love more practically in order to move into
this area of a joyful heart?

4. Commit to practicing the following: "I will resolve to love
others with the sacrificial love with which I have been loved
by God. I will seek to trust him to show his love through me
by practicing being a servant and lover of all those he has
place in my arena of life."

Dear heavenly Father,

It is often so hard for me to love some of those whom you have placed in my life, especially when I feel that I am giving of myself more than they are giving to me. Help me learn to practice love as Jesus showed me his love. Restore to me the joy that comes from extending your love to others. Thank you for always loving me, no matter what. I really want to abide always in your everlasting love. I love you. Amen.

Eight

Hearing the Refrain
of Heaven

On occasion, God lovingly wraps stories of eternity into the circumstances of my life, stories that seem to say, "I was here today." These jewels of his obvious presence are not trumpeted with horns and fanfare. They are usually slipped into the mundane and routine moments, yet they bring the eternal into view. God gave me such an experience during the early years of my marriage, through a special friendship.

Two months before Clay and I decided to get married, we attended a summer-long Christian student conference for leaders in Fort Collins, Colorado. While there, I met Marcy through a mutual acquaintance. She was thirty-three and engaged to be married the same month as our wedding. So of course we shared a friendship of mutual interest: marriage!

Throughout that summer we talked about our weddings and what they would be like, about the homes we would move into and how we would decorate them, and about all the other aspects of our lives that lay just ahead. Both of us got married that August, and by September, we had introduced our husbands to each other. Since we both lived in Denver, we would often go to each other's house for dinner or take in a movie together. We began to cultivate quite a friendship.

Six months later, Marcy and her husband moved out of town for her husband's job. Although we did not see each other as often, we still kept up our friendship. We spent time together whenever they came back to town and when we would make the three-hour drive to visit them. But since Clay was in seminary and carried a full class load and I was busily involved in my ministry work, we didn't get to spend as much time with our friends as we would have liked. Then distance took us even farther apart when Clay accepted a pastoral position in the International Chapel of Vienna, Austria. We would be gone for a year.

While I was overseas, a mutual friend wrote to tell me that Marcy had been diagnosed with ovarian cancer. My heart ached when I read the news. I knew how much Marcy wanted to have children, and this diagnosis meant she would probably never be able to. Worse, her mother had died of the same illness. Marcy had told me about the fear and dread she experienced as a child while watching her mom die.

I called her immediately. We prayed together over the phone, and I did my best to offer comfort. But I was amazed at her attitude. I had expected her to be devastated. Yet she was obviously trusting the Lord and doing all that she could to restore her health. I found that every time I called her, *I* ended up being encouraged. We corresponded as often as we could (these were the years just before e-mail or cell phones), and my year passed quickly. Clay and I returned to America just before Christmas of that year so that Clay could prepare for his final semester of seminary in January.

Upon returning home, I ran into another friend while shopping. "Sally, did you know that Marcy has taken a turn for the worse?" she told me. "They don't know if she's going to live more than a couple of months. Several of us are going together to visit her. We thought maybe it would encourage her to be with old friends. She asked if you could come."

Thankful for the opportunity to see Marcy face to face, I made arrangements to meet them the following week to carpool the three-hour drive together. The day before our trip, my friend called and said, "Marcy called me and asked if each of us would bring a big basket full of salad makings and bread. She said she would love for us to share a meal with her. And she said to bring a lot, so maybe she wants us to help her stock up since cooking is so hard for her right now."

The next morning arrived, and I found myself feeling uneasy about the visit. I had heard that Marcy had lost forty pounds (on her already thin frame) and most of her hair. And the aggressive chemotherapy had left her very weak. Even with the dread of what I would see, though, I did so want to be with my sweet friend.

Five of us (all friends who had gone to that providential training conference) piled into one car with our baskets filled with homemade breads, salads, desserts, and anything else we could think of that might bring some comfort to her. The drive passed quickly as we all caught up on life. When we neared Marcy's home, though, the atmosphere in the car changed. We weren't sure what to expect.

Marcy lived with her husband on a farm several miles outside of the closest town where she attended church and shopped. So there wouldn't be a lot of traffic. But as we approached her home, we found twenty to thirty cars parked down her country lane.

"I wonder if something's happened to her," one of my friends speculated. "I wonder if she died and people from her church have come to comfort her husband."

The dread in the pit of my stomach grew.

It is better to light one candle than to curse the darkness.

CHINESE PROVERB

AN ETERNAL PERSPECTIVE BRINGS PRESENT JOY

We exited the car feeling unsure, concerned about what we would find. We piled on her porch together and rang the doorbell. A few minutes later, the door opened and there was Marcy holding tightly to the doorjamb to keep from falling. Her balding head with pixie-straight tufts of hair; her too big, bright blue eyes; and her skinny body made her look a little like an elf. Covered in a floor-length green and red skirt, she appeared to be in party clothes ready to attend a Christmas gala.

A perky smile filled the hollows of her face, and her eyes sparkled with mischief. She leaned out the door and whispered, "Hi, my best friends. I'm so glad you're here. I hope you don't mind, but I decided I didn't want to waste your trip out to see me. I felt like having a real Christmas party. So I invited about thirty of my friends for a luncheon. Most of them don't know the Lord and are living terrible lives. I knew you were all great cooks, and so you're providing the meal. I told my friends to come for a great time with good food and fun and that I would provide the entertainment. By the way, you're my entertainment."

I imagine we all looked a bit surprised at that comment, but she continued describing her plans.

"I want each of you to tell your story about how you came to love Jesus. I would dearly love for all of my friends to be with me in heaven, and I knew that you could tell them how to get there. I'm too tired to do much speaking, but I just knew you would do this for me and make this a memorable day! I'm sorry I didn't tell you or my husband. I knew you all would just make me stay in bed—and that would be such a waste of your time with me, when we could be doing kingdom work. So please don't be mad. Just come in and have fun with me, and let's make one more memory!"

What amazement we felt that our friend, though diminished in body, was soaring in spirit. Of course, none of us wanted to disappoint her expectations, since she was being so incredibly noble.

A party atmosphere filled the house. Marcy had tables set up all over her dining room, living room, and hallway. Christmas lights blinked and sparkled in every place, and the room was filled with women laughing, talking, and having all sorts of girl fun. Baskets of a variety of salads and bread overflowed the buffet table, and everybody piled their plates high. Sweet Marcy settled into a wheelchair and beamed at the success of her plan. When we had eaten, the five of us shared our different stories of how we found Christ. We then told of how we had met Marcy at a Christian conference, where we were all leaders working with people to tell them how they could know Christ's love.

"Now I get to tell my story! It's my house and my party!" Marcy said.

She related how her mother had died of ovarian cancer many years before and how it had thrust her into depression as a girl. She went on to describe how a friend told her about heaven, the place of perfect beauty where Jesus will welcome all his children who love him, where there will be no more tears, where he's building us each a mansion.

"So when I go to meet him," she said, "I'll get to see my mom again and invite her into my mansion. And I want all of you to be with me, so I want to close by telling you how you can be sure."

By this time, there was not a dry eye in the house! Marcy shared a simple gospel presentation and closed in prayer. I am sure many of those women will be in heaven because of her wonderful party.

When the other women left, we had heart-to-hearts with Marcy. She said, "The hardest thing is the chemotherapy and the pain. Sometimes I get discouraged and feel deep darkness hovering in my soul. But I have realized that if I really believe in Jesus, then I will soon be relieved of all this pain and suffering. But it also means that I have a short time left to celebrate the Lord on this side of eternity. I want every day to be joyful, a celebration of the love I have for others, making memories, and not worrying about all the mundane things that I have wasted too much time on. And I want all of you to know that you are one of my most joyful memories. I love you so much!"

Somehow, Marcy had filled our emotional cups, inspired our faith, and left us feeling that we had all been in the presence of our Lord. Her perspective was eternal. She was holding on to hope, dancing to the music she heard so clearly inside her soul, which gave her an expectation of bringing a smile to the face of her beloved Savior. The brightness of her spirit overwhelmed the fragility of her body. We all left in peace.

Over the next weeks, Marcy and I talked often. Two months later, however, I received a call from our mutual friend. "Sally, Marcy isn't doing well at all. They don't know if she'll make it through the weekend. You'd better go visit her."

My last memory of Marcy took place in the hospital room where she died. She was so weak, she could not lift her head from the pillow. But the smile of her heart immediately covered her face as I walked into the room. Through a raspy voice, she quietly choked out to the nurse, "I told you my special friend was coming. She is one of the ones who knows how to give great parties and celebrate life with me. We have always made great memories together. Now be sure to listen to the story that I want her to tell you. I want you to be in heaven with me because you have taken such good care of me. So listen to Sally and do what she says, and I'm just going to close my eyes for a few minutes and rest. I'm a little tired."

Marcy had grasped the reality of heaven so clearly that she conquered her illness even though it ravaged her body. She understood that she had one chance to live in such a way that she would make the reality of God, his love, beauty, and redemption so real to others that they would want to know him and be with him too. She suffered a lot, and she endured excruciating pain. But she was never surprised at it, as she had accepted suffering as a part of life when her mother had died. Rather than letting it dictate how she would live, she focused on eternity. She danced with all of her being in such a way that she spread the music and life of God everywhere she went. It left an indelible mark on my life just to be near her. Her story and my memories of her life still bring me courage.

> Consider Him who has endured such hostility
> by sinners against Himself, so that you will
> not grow weary and lose heart.
>
> HEBREWS 12:3

THE MYSTERY OF JOY IN THE MIDST OF PAIN

One of the biggest puzzles for me has been understanding how to deal with suffering and yet have joy at the same time. This is a big subject and hardly one I can deal with comprehensively in one small chapter, but I do want to at least touch on this important question.

Being born with a strong sense of justice has made it difficult for me to understand why so much suffering happens to good people at the hands of bad people. Yet in reading Scripture and pondering life, I have realized that in order for me to have joy and hold God's hand in this dance of life, I have to mount up over these questions. The seeming inconsistencies of unanswered prayer, sickness, broken relationships, sin that corrupts and destroys, and all those consequences of life that tear our hearts apart are not to be dealt with in this world. If I am to dance, I do so by holding God's hand in faith, celebrating that he will, in time, judge the world and all its peoples and issues and bring justice for his children.

So as I began to examine joy in this context, I was not seeking to deal with the "why" of difficulty. That was a given. Instead I was seeking out the reality of how to live with joy in the midst of the sadness and death.

In Hebrews this very issue is the centerpiece. Consider these verses from Hebrews 12:1–2:

> Therefore, since we have so great a cloud of witnesses surrounding us, let us also lay aside every encumbrance and the sin which so easily entangles us, and let us run with endurance the race that is set before us, fixing our eyes on Jesus, the author and perfecter of faith, who for the joy set before Him endured the cross, despising the shame, and has sat down at the right hand of the throne of God.

The writer of Hebrews compared our lives to a race of endurance, a race in which joy is connected to what lies ahead, not to what is here right now. Just before these verses, in chapter 11, he called us to remember all of those who have gone before us who ran their race and finished well. The author listed the "Hall of Faith" and recounted the stories in Scripture of people who lived lives of faith and succeeded in pleasing God—the heroes of the faith. They are the cloud of witnesses who have gone before us. His admonition was for us to lay aside every encumbrance and sin, which so easily entangles us, in order to run this race of life with endurance.

Next he admonished us to fix our eyes on Jesus. Jesus is our target— the focal point of our lives and the finishing line of our faith. In other words, if we are to run well, we need to look at what Jesus did, follow his example, and run with his presence every step so that he can perfect our faith. Jesus endured the suffering of the cross because his eyes were on the "joy set before Him." I believe that the "joy set before Him" was the ultimate redemption of mankind through his sacrifice for us on the cross. He also took joy in knowing that he would soon be back with his Father, ruling and honored in the heavenlies as the Prince of peace, when he would once again "sit down at the right hand of the throne of God."

Jesus, once again our model for joy, endured the suffering because he knew that redemption and reward were coming. This must be the motivation of our lives if we are to experience internal joy in the midst of suffering: the certainty that we will be rewarded and justified in heaven because of our faith in his promise to make a place for us, the confidence that one day we will be in a place where there are no more tears. We can fix our eyes on Jesus, the One who is cheering us on, praying for us, waiting to greet us at the finish line of life.

I love the passage in Revelation that describes a part of the reality of heaven for us: " 'And He will wipe away every tear from their eyes; and there will no longer be any death; there will no longer be any mourning, or crying, or pain; the first things have passed away.' And He who sits on the throne said, 'Behold, I am making all things new.' And He said, 'Write, for these words are faithful and true' " (Revelation 21:4–5).

IT'S NATURAL TO DESPISE PAIN

To dance in the midst of terrible suffering is to resolve, "I will not be a victim. I will not allow this situation to determine the response of my heart, because I have this life, this chance to trust God, to show his reality through my circumstances. I resolve to remain strong and faithful because of the loving God who holds my hand."

One more amazing phrase from Hebrews 12:1–2 gave me great encouragement. As I read and contemplated these verses, I was struck by a few words poked into the middle of the passage: "despising the shame."

Even though Jesus focused on the joy he would experience at a later time, even though he stood confidently in what would take place in the future, he still "despised the shame." In other words, even though Jesus held on to the joy, he still disdained, despised, *hated,* felt terrible about the shame he was going through.

When I experience pain or sadness or anger at the cruelty of life, I am relating to the feelings of Jesus. He despised the pain; he felt it, bore it, struggled through it. In his humanity, Jesus felt the anguish poignantly. He has not asked us to experience any depth of suffering that he himself has not already endured.

This tells me that just because we feel sadness or disappointment or great sorrow doesn't mean we are not trusting God. If Jesus felt fully the ramifications of his horrible death, then it is normal for us to resist the pain, to dislike the suffering. It is a natural response to difficulty and injustice. God prewired us with the ability to discern between what is pleasurable and what is sad. Our emotional health is dependent on our ability to feel, deal with, and synthesize these varying emotions.

But it is our ultimate focus on the hope that is beyond that will pull us out of the cloud of our dark emotions into the light of his promises of future joy. This requires us to exercise our will and discipline our minds. We must place our thoughts on Scripture and stand in its truth. No one else can fight this battle and accomplish this victory for us. Yet I am convinced that the God who sees every hidden moment considers these to be faith offerings of our heart. That even in the midst of our suffering, he sees some of the greatest works of our lives: our belief, our assurance of things hoped for, our convictions of those things we cannot see.

Only by responding to God and worshiping him through faith will we arrive at that place of victory and overwhelming joy. This is the faith that pleases God. I have discovered that when I exercise this faith, my heart becomes filled with joy. It is the joy of knowing and sensing his pleasure. It is a joy that acts as a seal to the faith I have committed in quiet resolve to him. There is an internal joy, too, an intangible assurance that what I am doing is true and right and good.

King David validated this truth in Psalm 30:5: "Weeping may last for the night, but a shout of joy comes in the morning." We wait for the night to pass. And again, Psalms tells us that "those who sow in tears shall reap with joyful shouting" (Psalm 126:5). We must keep sowing through our tears. But we have the hope that our tears will be turned to joy.

> Those who sow in tears shall reap with joyful shouting.
> He who goes to and fro weeping, carrying his bag
> of seed, shall indeed come again with a shout of joy,
> bringing his sheaves with him.
>
> PSALM 126:5-6

WHEN YOU REALLY NEED THERE TO BE A HEAVEN

Maturity in our spiritual lives is a process of growth, an increasing understanding of applied wisdom. So my own growth in understanding how to experience joy in the midst of suffering has been a slow but steady process of transferring what I know to how I live. I'm so thankful that, while God is faithful to show me from his Word the theological framework supporting these concepts and truths, he always gives me the stories of real-life people to show me what the truth looks like when lived out.

These lessons started when I moved overseas to do missions work. I was young and idealistic and had not suffered much, so I was unable to exhibit the joy God wanted me to experience. Dancing with him, even as a young woman new to the journey, required me to embrace his goodness when I could not feel it. By faith, I held his hand with the confidence that he would lead me to a broader understanding as I walked these paths with him.

I didn't realize just how "American" I was until I moved to Europe to work with students. I was a twenty-four-year-old who had grown up in a country where freedom is a foundational expectation. Consequently, I bristled whenever I had to cross the borders from a free country in Western Europe, such as Austria, into a Communist country such as Hungary, Czechoslovakia, Poland, Romania, and Yugoslavia. These were the main countries where I first worked and traveled as a young missionary.

In Western countries, our passports received a cursory glance. In the Communist block countries, however, our papers were checked, our luggage was checked, and even at times they would pull out my car seat to see if I was carrying contraband, such as Bibles or biblical study guides. Once, my roommate and I were even called in to be questioned by the police.

"You have applied for a visa to leave our country to visit Western Europe," the officer said suspiciously. (We left every six months to go to Vienna for a little break from our difficult existence.) "I want to know where you are going, who you are going to visit, and what will be your business."

Indignation filled my heart. "What right do you have to question me?" I told him. "I'm an American citizen, and I have my freedoms!"

"I don't care if you are the president of the United States," he replied. "You are in my country, and I have jurisdiction over you. I can ask you anything I so desire. Now, tell me where you will be staying and what your business is there."

We gave a generalized answer to appease him without giving away any information that would point to our association with our mission group.

This was just a small beginning to my seeing life from a different point of view. Often on our trips, we would speak in small, run-down, crowded apartments to people sitting on every chair, every inch of floor, and in every room, hallway, and space. These wonderful believers would do anything, including walking many miles, just to hear the Word of God taught. Many had husbands imprisoned for their faith and children who had been questioned. Others had lost their jobs because they were believers. The government had ways of punishing the people who believed in God so that they would think twice before spreading the gospel to someone else.

Yet I was amazed at their hearts filled with joy and thanksgiving. Often our mission hosted small conferences in farmers' houses or barns hidden away from the secret police. The people would always sing loudly and fervently, thanking God for his love and graciousness. Of course they felt pain, fear, and suffering, and I saw many tears and much sadness for their oppression. But there was a palpable joy and hope in their demeanor, both personally and corporately.

When I puzzled over this, a stooped, silver-haired woman gently put her hand on mine and said, "When you really need there to be a heaven and when you believe in it with all your heart, you have great reason to rejoice because you know this life is so short. You count on the fact that you will live forever in a place that you were designed for from the beginning of the world. The problem is that, sometimes, you who live in the Western world have so much of heaven on earth, with all of your things and relative security and stability, that you can't clearly see the world that is ahead. And often, I think, you don't feel as much of a need for heaven." She patted my hand. "The one who can clearly understand why heaven will be such a place of blessing will never demand too much of life in a world that has been separated from God. We know from the shadows of beauty we see here that we were designed for a better place. It is for our joy in that very real fact that our hearts are full and that we sing so strongly."

And so, gently, Jesus began to loosen my grasp on what I wanted from this world to make me happy, to open my heart for what was ahead. Moving back to America where big houses fill almost all the cities, where things and "stuff" fill the horizon of our daily lives, and ease of life is an expectation, it became easy to sometimes forget the lessons of my earlier years. Yet as I have pondered these and other stories that God so faithfully placed into my life, I realized that he does not want me to be satisfied with second best—a world far separated from his original design. Instead, he faithfully showed me that only when I live for those things that are eternal will I be fitted for a heavenly kingdom.

For me, the lessons came through the details of my life story; those unanswerable issues that find no solutions. Miscarriages and near-death illness, three out of four severely asthmatic children, rejection from family members because of our ideals, church splits that caused brokenness and devastation, financial problems, marriage stresses. It often seemed that life presented me with more problems than solutions. Yet God was gently leading me to look for a life that would truly answer the longings for which I had originally been created. He gently broke my dependence on those things that could never satisfy. The choice to hold his hand through the dance of suffering resulted in greater emotional freedom. I learned to let go of temporal things more quickly, and the joy of just living and *being* with him through moments of my days became more real.

In remembering the lessons of the past I have once again found joy and freedom. As I have made time to search after joy, I have been able to remember all of the joyful paths he has already led me down, and again I am learning to savor each moment as one in which I can learn, grow, and love him more. Even now as I write while engaging with him, I am learning so much and my soul is growing in its capacity to be grateful for his showing me these truths in a gentle and loving way in the midst of today's burdens.

God has stepped into this world, into our lives, to assure us that we really can follow Jesus in enduring suffering for "the joy set before us," being in heaven with our Creator, our Father. This is the truth that Marcy knew and lived, dancing to the song of heaven, the eyes of her soul filled with the beauty of what was ahead. As she held fast to the hand of her Father, she followed the steps of the dance he taught her even through the valley of the shadow of death, celebrating the eternal life that will never end.

Finding *Your* Rhythm in God's Joy

1. The writer of Hebrews reminded us: "Fixing our eyes on Jesus…who for the joy set before Him endured the cross, despising the shame, and has sat down at the right hand of the throne of God. For consider Him who has endured such hostility by sinners against Himself, so that you will not grow weary and lose heart" (Hebrews 12:2–3).

   What does it mean to consider him, so that we may not grow weary and lose heart?

What is the joy set before you?

Is it necessarily wrong to grieve and feel sorrow in this life?

2. Read the prophecy about Jesus as foretold in Isaiah 53:3–4: "He was despised and forsaken of men, a man of sorrows and acquainted with grief; and like one from whom men hide their face He was despised, and we did not esteem Him. Surely our griefs He himself bore, and our sorrows He carried."

How do you think Jesus feels toward us since he bore our sorrows and carried our grief? If he felt the pain that you feel in your deepest pain, do you think he understands you and is ready to comfort you?

Jesus is our companion in the most difficult place of
our lives because he willingly bore our sorrows and
carried our grief. He entered into our pain. In prayer,
tell Jesus what is difficult for you and ask him to meet
you at your point of need.

3. Revelation 21:4–5 indicates a time when all our tears will
   be wiped away. What does this passage say there will be no
   more of?

   What hope does this give to us in our present
   sufferings?

   If you really believed what this verse says, how could
   that provide you joy now?

What ways are you counting on this world to be the place where you will get ultimate happiness?

When does the Bible say our lives will be painless? How should that change the way you live right now?

Dear precious Lord,

Help me to remember that my greatest joy is ahead—being in eternity in the presence of my King, in a place you have prepared for me. Give me strength to endure the crosses before me, even in the pain, for what I can see in the eyes of my heart lies ahead. Help me to yield all of my present sorrows to you in order to be freer in this life. Please help me to have the perspective of Jesus—for the joy set before me. Thank you for entering into my sorrows and for loving me. I love you. Amen.

Nine

Exchanging the Drudgery of Duty for the Dance of Delight

"I feel like God is so disappointed in me," my friend whispered between sobs. "No matter how hard I try or how much I give, it never feels like it's enough, and I don't know what to do."

At thirty-two years old, she found herself empty and worn out. After serving for many years as a counselor to troubled teens, she married a pastor of college students and opened her home to hundreds of youth who were looking for answers to life's questions. Then, in five years she had three boys and little sleep. The guilt and inadequacy that had been bubbling in her heart for many years was finally boiling to the surface.

She'd grown up in a wealthy home, where the expectations for her and her two brothers had been very high. She lived under constant threat of disappointing her demanding parents and longed for their approval. When she was seventeen, after many years of fighting, her parents got a divorce. The foundation of love in her life was further shaken. The devastation she had experienced prepared her to respond to Christ's love when she first heard the message at a youth rally.

Even though she became a solid, faithful Christian, she still carried the baggage from her youth. She believed that God, like her father, was

demanding and expected perfection from her. She held on to the lingering suspicion that she was in some way responsible for her parents'
divorce, since she often overheard them arguing about her siblings and
her. So she entered adulthood with an intense drive to please everyone—
her husband, her children, her parents, and anyone she met.

"There are so many needs in the world, and I find myself feeling
responsible for all of them! No matter how often I read the Bible or have
quiet times, God seems far away, and I know it's my fault. I don't know
if I'll ever be adequate enough or understand him," she said. Then she
laid her head on her arms and cried quietly.

I didn't mean to be distracted from her sorrow, but next to her was
her three-month-old, squishy, rosy-cheeked little baby boy smiling and
grinning at me every time I glanced down at him. It was almost impossible to ignore him—and he engagingly called for a response as he
grinned and did a jig with his little feet hanging off the end of his car seat.

"Kathryn," I said as I gently touched her arm. "Look at your darling,
irresistible little boy." He unwittingly drew a sheepish grin from her tear-
stained face. "How do you feel about him?"

"He's a bundle of fun and joy for all of us," she answered. "He brings
so much pleasure to my life every day."

"Why do you love him and stay up with him and nurse him and
change his diapers? Is it because he has been useful to you or worked for
you or accomplished great things?"

"I would do anything for him just because he's my precious little boy
and I adore him."

"That's exactly how the Lord feels about you. He has given you the
gift of this child to show you how much he adores you. You are his, and
he deeply loves you and will *always* care for you. It's not because you
deserve it or have accomplished any great thing. It's simply because he is
your heavenly Father."

She nodded slightly.

"Think about what David wrote in Psalm 103:13," I continued. " 'Just as a father has compassion on his children, so the LORD has compassion on those who fear Him.' He doesn't love you for your service. He responds to you because you are his child and he delights in your smiles. He is all loving, and he can't *not* love you—it's part of his nature."

HOW GOD CLOSES THE DISTANCE

How often I have felt as my friend did, weighed down by my emotional baggage, an inadequate view of God, and guilt from my own failures. I have met so many women who live out of fear and inadequacy. They transfer their feelings about themselves to God and then feel distant from him.

Julian of Norwich, a saint from church history, said, "This is the cause why we be not all in ease of heart and soul: that we seek here rest [and joy] in those things that are so little, wherein is no rest, and know not our God that is All-mighty, All-wise, All-good. For He is the Very Rest."[1]

No matter how hard we try, how many achievements we make, or how many ideals we keep, we will never be able to do enough to earn God's love. Such attempts lead us down a dead-end road paved with feelings of life-depleting guilt and condemnation. Only the grace and love that God gives freely through his merciful nature can provide us with that which we long for: peace and joy.

I was to learn this lesson through my fourth child, whom we providentially named Joy.

At forty-one years old, I had three children and enjoyed being a mom to them—at least most of the time. But I longed for another child. I'd had three miscarriages, one from which I almost bled to death and had to be transported to the hospital in an ambulance. Consequently, I was reluctantly adjusting my expectations about having any more babies. Clay was concerned about my health. So in a difficult moment, I agreed to sell our baby stuff and my maternity clothes at a garage sale. We decided to move on and enjoy the children God had given us.

My youngest child, six-year-old Nathan, came to me one day and said, "Mama, I don't think you should give up on having one more baby. I think God wants us to have another baby girl. You do believe in prayer, don't you?"

"Of course I do, Nathan, but Mama's getting older and my body just doesn't work like it used to."

"Will you at least pray with me about it, just a little bit?" he almost demanded.

It was not long until his prayers were answered! I found myself throwing up in the mornings just six weeks later! The incidents of the frightening miscarriages had me worried. I would be just shy of forty-two years old when this baby arrived. I was also concerned because we were scheduled to perform in a musical production on the life of Christ in the Kremlin Palace Theater in Moscow just at the week when I'd had my miscarriages in my previous pregnancies. The thought of having a miscarriage in a Russian hospital scared me. Over the next weeks, I visited the doctor, and he seemed to think this baby was here to stay. So off to Russia we went. My baby was taken all over the stage, swinging and swirling to music as she grew inside of me. In one short week, we performed twelve times. (I think that my being on stage influenced her, as she came out being a ham!)

Several more months passed. When I reached thirty weeks, I started to have premature labor pains. Once again, I wondered if this little baby would be born healthy and whole. By week thirty-two, my doctor placed me on bed rest for at least six more weeks. Every time I had a labor pain, I would pray for this baby to wait. In the midst of my difficulties, a sweet friend came to see me. Just before she left my house, she put her hand on my very big belly, patted it, and said, "You know, Sally, every time I pray for this baby, I call her Baby Joy." And then she prayed for Baby Joy to be healthy and strong.

The rest of the pregnancy we called this baby "Baby Joy." Finally at the dinner table one evening, one of the kids commented that since we had called this baby "Joy" for so long, maybe that's what we should call her. So Joy it was. The Lord does have a sense of humor, though. After I stayed in bed obediently so that she wouldn't come early, she was the only child I had who came two weeks *late*.

But finally, Joy entered the world, and from the moment of her birth, she lived up to her name.

A child sings before it speaks, dances almost before
it walks. Music is in our hearts from the beginning.

PAMELA BROWN

A FULLY ENGAGED HEART

Sometimes when I look back over the fourteen years of Joy's life, I almost feel as though the Lord meant for me to name her Joy as a symbol that joy would become a quest for my heart. He has even used my daughter to teach me about biblical joy just through the antics of her life.

During eight weeks of bed rest, I'd had plenty of time to think about this baby before she arrived. At my age and after three miscarriages, I hadn't dared hope the Lord would to give me another chance to have a sweet baby, let alone another little girl. So I knew what a blessing this child was. I was granted one more opportunity to love a little baby, to nurse her, and to sing and rock her to sleep. The loss of the other babies enhanced my appreciation of this precious gift.

Patience came more easily with this baby because I was better prepared, after my first three, for the challenges of infancy. Because she was a gift I never expected to receive, I found I didn't mind the hours I would nurse her. I didn't see them as an intrusion to my life, because I knew she would be my last.

All of us enjoyed her funny ways and loved just watching her be a baby. My other children had been just as miraculous, but we valued her as a treasure because we knew that apart from this miracle, we would never have had her. God opened the eyes of our hearts to really see the gift of a baby. And so in her, our joy as a family was full—much fuller than when having babies was a given.

Joy's habit of placing her foot in her mouth and sucking on her toes at five months seemed especially hysterical to my children. Her cooing and swaying back and forth to the rhythm of singing and music delighted our other children and prompted them to sing back to her. Hearing her giggle with a deep belly laugh every time our dog licked her little hand made us all giggle. While similarly wonderful moments had taken place with my other babies, I had often neglected to see them, to participate in them, or to connect with them, because I was distracted by the responsibilities of life. I now realized how much I had missed with my previous babies because I had been distracted with my own agenda. I had missed out on so much joy.

A meteorite shower was expected one evening, so our family gathered in sleeping bags out on our deck to watch. Countless stars blinked and twinkled as we shivered in the cold mountain evening, cuddled together underneath our sleeping bags. We gazed at the brightness of the evening sky in a quiet hush.

Little Joy, having just celebrated her fourth birthday, was wrapped in her beloved "blanky," snuggled up close to me on my pillow. She said, "How could any smart person not believe in Dod [God], if they could see all these twinkly, pretty lights he decorated the sky with just to make us happy?"

Time seemed to stop at moments like these, because the eyes of my heart were opened to the joy of life seen through the eyes of innocence. The blessing of this precious child, and the painful reality that she would likely be my last, fashioned in my soul a fresh sensitivity, an ability to see beauty that had been there all along but often had remained unnoticed. Through Baby Joy, God helped me cultivate an awareness of blissful moments, which filled the cup of my heart to overflowing. I began to engage my heart in this search for hidden treasure. I looked for the shadows of his ways and the evidence of his signature along every step of my life. In some ways, I felt I had been given a second chance, a new opportunity to live fully engaged in the melody his Spirit was singing to me.

When I intentionally asked God to open my eyes to his provision of joy, I began to notice even small, everyday occurrences as a gift, such as the sunrise and sunset. I can often look out my bedroom window, which has a view over the tops of pine trees, and see the majestic navy blue mountains of Colorado. Before I take up the vigil to pray for my burdens, I have learned to stop first in order to notice God or to praise him or to ask him what he wants me to see. Most days I am greeted by pinks and blues and purples—a gift of joyful color with which to see and praise the Lord. I take this as a personal morning message that God is present to give delight and beauty to this day. Then I'm reminded of the Scripture that says, "From the rising of the sun to its setting the name of the LORD is to be praised" (Psalm 113:3). Or the psalm that declares, "The Mighty One, God, the LORD, has spoken, and summoned the earth from the rising of the sun to its setting" (50:1).

I mentally stop what I am busy "doing" to notice for a few seconds the fact that God has painted the sky and flowers and trees for our pleasure. I picture him as a Father ready to show me the wonders he has prepared. I have come to call these moments "joy anchors." God has strewn over my life small grace moments, when an encouraging word from a friend or an article I have read reminds me of his presence and provision. But I need to *notice* them in order for him to fill me with his joy. As I have asked God to open the eyes of my heart so I can see like my little child, I have glimpsed his Spirit dancing in my life, painting beauty, love, and joy in the midst of the mundane.

HOLDING ON TO WORRY

Watching how my daughter responded to life taught me a lot of lessons.

When overwhelmed by my circumstances, I learned to pray, "God, here are our bills that seem too many. In your time, show us how you will provide. Father, I am lonely and weary today, but you know that. Please strengthen me. Lord, you see the heart of my rebellious teen. You have access to his mind and heart. Please speak to him today." Whatever the need, I would give it to him. Then I would open my eyes in innocent expectation, which I learned from observing baby Joy. It has served to put me and my life more into the perspective of a bigger God, who is above my limited circumstances. I am not minimizing the larger and more demanding issues of my life. But by focusing on the transcendence of God, his power, presence, and character, I put the problems of life in their proper place.

Another lesson came when Joy was just beyond toddlerhood. Her bedroom was next to Clay's and mine. When Joy was old enough to climb out of her bed, she would toddle into our room between 5:00 and 6:00 a.m. and climb into bed with me. She would just lift my covers, squeeze in next to me, and throw her leg over my body (as if to lock me into position!). Within seconds, she would be breathing heavily, at peace in a deep sleep. I loved her sweet little frame next to mine.

One morning as I was cherishing this closeness, I realized that Joy took comfort from me because she knew her relationship with me was secure. Knowing I loved and cherished her, that I would provide for her as I had always provided, and that I was her protector, she came naturally to where she knew she belonged. As my daughter, she knew she had the right to come cuddle in next to me. She never asked, "Mommy, have I been good enough to get in bed with you? Or have I done enough work to get in bed with you?" Those are the very attitudes we carry, which often separate us from coming to God as his own children. She didn't let these issues become barriers because she felt unselfconscious and unhindered. She just expected me to love her because I was her mother.

It dawned on me that often I allow the trappings of this world and the clouds of my day to get in the way of crawling into my heavenly Father's arms. It was during this period that Psalm 131:1–2 became dear to me:

Oh, LORD, my heart is not proud, nor my eyes haughty;
Nor do I involve myself in great matters,
Or in things too difficult for me.
Surely I have composed and quieted my soul;
Like a weaned child rests against his mother,
My soul is like a weaned child within me.

Until I am willing to come to him as a little child with all my issues, big and small, I may not feel free enough to dance to his rhythms. If I don't let go of the burdens and hold on to his hand, my joy will be stolen as I bear the worries and burdens that God has offered to shoulder for me.

I have realized that when I worry about every responsibility I carry, if I stress over each potential problem, I quench the Holy Spirit who is within me. He desires to hold these burdens for me, to quiet my soul. I can either have joy in dancing freely, letting my heavenly Father lead and hold me, or I can bear all my burdens myself. But it is not possible to do both at the same time. This becoming like a child is a subtle way of turning my heart toward life and toward my heavenly Father, of releasing my tight hold on the things that seem so big and frightening and worrisome in order to hold on to his loving hand.

Often, when I have very little margin in my life, I notice that I become less patient, more self-centered and demanding. Although Jesus always had people following him and making demands of him, he still made time for prayer with his Father and time to develop close relationships with his disciples. Watching the simplicity of Jesus' life has taught me little by little to do what I can do for *this* moment and complete what I can for *this* day, then go to bed and sleep restfully, not borrowing trouble from the next day for all the things I haven't completed. I adjust my expectations to the realities of my life. I seek not to lose or abuse opportunities to love and enjoy those who are precious to me.

However, this letting go of burdens does not come naturally to me. I have had to resolve not to carry them. The dictionary lists several definitions for *resolve* that, added together, describe what I have committed to in my heart: to come to a firm decision; to find a solution to a problem; to dispel doubts or anxiety and move ahead in a confident conclusion. I mentally give these burdens to God through prayer when my spirit feels the quick darts of fear, anxiety, and irritation. By an act of my will, I acknowledge to the Lord that I do not want to be guided by negative emotions. I leave them there in his capable hands, then I move forward into the day, seeking to enjoy each person in my life as a blessing, not focusing on our stresses or differences or my inadequacies but letting his love cover "a multitude of sins" (1 Peter 4:8) and remembering that "love…is the perfect bond of unity" (Colossians 3:14).

By practicing this, I have slowly come to see that my inner being is changing; I am able to go through the days without the weight of life always bearing down on me. It has required me to notice when darkness descends over my mood and then identify the issue or thought or circumstance that produced this anxiety or stress. When I identify the root of my unease, I can resolutely turn it over to the Lord, mentally leave it there, and ask for him to restore my peace. It is a discipline, a practice that slowly eliminates those issues that rob me of joy and separate me from him.

Though you have not seen Him, you love Him, and though you do not see Him now, but believe in Him, you greatly rejoice with joy inexpressible and full of glory.

1 PETER 1:8

LEAVE FOR TODAY WHAT IS TODAY'S

It was because of these issues related to anxiety, worry, and weariness that I came to study joy to begin with. I am convinced that many of my godly colleagues, with whom I have worked and observed on the mission field, have repeatedly taken their burdens and unanswerable questions into their own hands and so quenched the Holy Spirit's fruit in their lives. As I observed the result, how it drained them of life and passion, I began to ponder how to live and die with a joyful heart. And I learned that part of the answer lies in doing what I can today to sort through the piles of life and leave the rest until the morrow.

As I picture Joy sleeping peacefully in my arms when she was a baby, I envision myself resting in the strong hands of my Father. I trust my able dance partner to lead me capably through each song, confident that he knows where he is taking me. I choose always to remember the attributes that I love about him: that he is good and will lead me in goodness; that he loves me as a good Shepherd and in that role, he will protect and care for me; that he is my loving Father and will love and provide for me.

These acts of remembrance are a sort of love offering, which helps me participate in the dance with love and appreciation for my partner. It connects my heart to his and brings me a growing sense of pleasure and enjoyment in each special moment. Instead of stooping under a burden of darkness piling up formidably on the shoulders of my soul, I move freely, knowing that my burdens are being carried by one stronger and more capable than I.

Though I do not want to belabor this point, I will try to explain what it looks like just a little more clearly. By not involving "myself...in things too difficult for me" (Psalm 131:1) when I face a problem that brings fear, worry, and stress beyond my ability to control, I make a concerted effort to pray those things to God. I tell him my thoughts, the extent of my worry, the depths of my despair, and then I intentionally visualize placing it all before his throne, where I know he rules the universe.

Just this morning, I had to take Joy to a drama camp, leaving the house at 8:00 a.m. My husband, Clay, came to me just as I was going out the door to ask about an upcoming ministry commitment for which I need to prepare twenty-four distinct eighteen-minute talks for a video production—and I haven't even started! My son Joel called while I was starting the car to say that he is out of money. He has a lead on a possible job, but he needed me to e-mail the information about the loan package that I had cosigned for him. As I got on the freeway, the traffic was bumper to bumper.

Sometimes on mornings like this, I feel my body get tense. I become anxious and fret. But today I deliberately chose to let each stress roll off my back into the hands of my Father. "I will not involve myself in things too difficult for me," I prayed. "Thank you that you are capable of leading me through this obstacle course of life. Thank you for this beautiful Colorado day. Help me to walk it with you."

Making a choice to resist stewing and fretting over all the issues of my day gives me the ability to delight in each moment as a gift. I give each morning into the Father's hands and picture myself more and more at rest against him like a weaned child. By faith, I take my place next to him, counting on him to care for me and protect me and to accept me as I am—even with my limitations—because of his grace and because of my role as his daughter. My responsibilities have not changed, but my *relationship* to my responsibilities has. They are not mine to hold; they are his. I work hard when I am able, play intentionally, rest regularly, love purposefully, and seek to make each day count.

Growing older has also given me fresh perspective. Every season of life seems to bring its own dilemmas. Yet as I look back, I can see that I lived through all of them, that he used each circumstance to teach me more about life and about him, and that I am still moving ahead. I also know that I will never be perfect, that controlling life is an impossible and unreasonable goal. Eternity with God has become more precious to me as I have allowed him to take my hold on those things that really do not matter, to gently place each of my fingers into the palm of his hand, to feel his grasp on my hand, confidently leading me forward.

This sounds a little Pollyannaish, but it is not. Over the years and especially the last months of mentally assenting to this way of life, God has increased my capacity to work more, give more, and live more efficiently in relationship to the myriad responsibilities he has brought my way. As I learn to rest in his strength and care, I am in many ways able to have more on my plate. I have seen that it is not the work load or busyness of people that causes them to be joyful or not; it is the way they live within the limitations and responsibilities that are on their plate. Being childlike is not just doing nothing, but it *is* resting in him.

As I was studying my Bible recently, I ran across two more verses that caused me to ponder my part in cultivating a child-heart. Both seem to focus on a similar thought. The first passage was the scene when Jesus sent out seventy followers to preach the gospel. As he sent them, he said, "I send you out as lambs in the midst of wolves" (Luke 10:3). This statement caught my attention because lambs are a picture of innocence and wolves are evil predators. Jesus said the disciples were being sent out as lambs. He didn't require them to be savvy or sophisticated. Later in the passage when they returned with great stories of what happened when they preached, Jesus' response was, "I praise you, O Father, Lord of heaven and earth, that You have hidden these things from the wise and intelligent and have revealed them to [little children]. Yes, Father, for this way was well-pleasing in Your sight" (verse 21).

The disciples, who were known for their love, passion, and devotion to Jesus, were the "children" he was talking about. It was God's good pleasure to choose these simple, plain, working-class men—as they were like children in their openness to Jesus. Their hearts were open to see and believe in him.

Their sincerity made a stark contrast to the Pharisees and Sadducees, who were more educated, wealthy, and sophisticated. Measuring spirituality by legalistic formulas, these leaders of the Jewish synagogue made life burdensome for all who knew them. Jesus had some harsh words for the Pharisees: *vipers* (Matthew 12:24–34), *blind* (15:12–14), *hypocrites* (23:13–19), *serpents* (23:33), *children of the devil* (John 8:13, 44). These were Israel's leaders he was talking about! Their confidence was bound up in their belief system rather than in the One who was their Creator, Redeemer, and Provider—Jesus, who called himself the Way, the Truth, and the Life (14:6). *He* was their pathway to God, but they chose their systems instead.

They felt no need for him because they were filled up with themselves. They quoted the Law and rules they made connected to the Torah, but their lives were not about devotion and love for God or for those around them who needed God's compassion and redemption. For all their "knowledge" and religion, the Pharisees were not who Jesus chose to lead his people; instead he chose the disciples and others who followed him, calling them "lambs" and "children."

Jesus himself came to the world in simplicity. No palace, servants, status, or wealth. His authority came from within. He commanded attention because of his insight, love, and compassion for the "undesirables"—the prostitutes, fishermen, tax collectors, outcasts, women, and children—the commoners. And these humble folk who were demeaned by the Pharisees were those who "turned the world upside down" (Acts 17:6, KJV).

CULTIVATING A CHILD-HEART

Jesus was "childlike," innocent, free from the trappings of his culture's expectations, pure in heart to see into the hearts of men. Understanding this about him helped me realize that if I come to him in sincere love, humility, trust, and worship, then I will *really* see him more clearly. The joy of God can only flow through our lives when we relate with integrity to God.

Again, the Lord used Joy to help me better understand this concept. One day, when she was about three years old, I was rocking her and singing softly to her before putting her down for a nap. She looked into my eyes and asked, "Mommy, why do all those men put Jesus on a cross and kill him? It makes me so sad because he was the singer to children and he loved them."

Joy had acted with me in *The Promise,* a production about the life of Christ, which our family was involved in for three years, six months a year. So she had gone with me on stage every Friday and Saturday evening and witnessed the play firsthand. She even eventually developed a part all by herself in which every night Jesus would touch her as he was singing and walking through the crowds. She learned to smile at him and extend her little hand to touch him as he passed her way. It was definitely a crowd pleaser. Because this story was real to her from being in the midst of it for sixty-five performances, at home she would pretend that she was Mary and hold her little dolls and call them "Jesus." So I was not surprised at her talking to me about the story.

"It seems so sad that they would kill Jesus and be so mean to him," Joy remarked seriously. "Didn't they know he was the One who loved them the most? He was the One who sang the best songs and even liked all the children. I think the most important thing is to love him back and to make his eyes smile. If they just did that, there wouldn't be any more problems and no one would be mean anymore."

Her innocent, fresh, and intelligent mind grasped the injustice of Jesus' violent death. Her desire to believe in and to please this Savior was heartfelt and uncomplicated.

And so in relationship to my sweet little girl, this verse became dear to my heart. "Whoever then humbles himself as this child, he is the greatest in the kingdom of heaven" (Matthew 18:4).

A similar passage was also special. When children had been brought to Jesus to be blessed, his disciples told them to go away. But he reacted in a way that surprised everyone: "When Jesus saw this, He was indignant and said to them, 'Permit the children to come to Me; do not hinder them; for the kingdom of God belongs to such as these. Truly I say to you, whoever does not receive the kingdom of God like a child will not enter it at all.' And He took them in His arms and began blessing them, laying His hands on them" (Mark 10:14–16).

As I rocked Joy and listened to her little sermon, these words kept echoing in my mind, *Whoever does not receive the kingdom of God like a child will not enter it at all.* Joy didn't complicate her mind with questions or thorny issues; she just saw Jesus for who he is: the Savior, the Creator, the Source of love.

Over the years I have seen many people, both prominent Christians and everyday believers, wrangle about words and doctrines and ideals. And yet these definitive doctrines that so often captivate the mind rarely seem to penetrate the *heart* of those debating over them.

Of course, the doctrines and Scriptures of the Bible are our foundation upon which to stand. I am not suggesting we ignore our intellect. My own study of Scripture and attending seminary classes have built a foundation of knowledge for me as I have studied for forty years. But all of our study must have the eventual effect of causing us to worship God, to fall deeply in love with Jesus as we understand his humility and power, his justice and grace, his wisdom and obedience to the Father.

Just as a child so generously and wholeheartedly trusts in one who is true, we must demonstrate sincere devotion to the One who leads us in the dance of our lives. And so it was a child named Joy whom God used to bring me back to the essentials and to help me understand him more clearly. Joy led me to release myself to the dance I had been designed to experience—as a child, relinquishing all of life's distractions and joyfully swirling in the pleasure of the One who would take me ably through his dance, the One who shows his pleasure by assuring me of his love and helping me release myself to the fullness of his gladness.

Finding *Your* Rhythm in God's Joy

1. Psalm 103:13–14 says, "Just as a father has compassion on his children, so the LORD has compassion on those who fear Him. For He Himself knows our frame; He is mindful that we are but dust." According to this verse, is God aware of our fragility and limitations? Does he expect more from us than we can give?

   What kind of compassion do you think a good father would have for his children?

   In what ways have you tried to earn God's acceptance?

   Write down any failures or sins you have committed that you think God has held against you. Write across the paper, "Forgiven and loved" and then tear the paper and throw it away—as an act of accepting his love and grace.

2. Psalm 131:1–2 says, "Nor do I involve myself in great matters.... I have composed and quieted my soul." What are the things in your life that are "too great" that you have been trying to handle?

   What would it look like for you to give these areas over to God?

   How can you still and quiet your soul?

3. What does it mean, "Unless you are converted and become like children, you will not enter the kingdom of heaven" (Matthew 18:3)? How does a child exercise belief differently from an adult?

Adults usually require proof before they will trust in anything. Does God want us to provide for our own needs or depend on him to provide? What would that look like in your life?

How do you need to change your heart attitude in order to more fully enjoy God's Fatherhood?

4. Commit to simplifying your life and seeking God with the innocent heart of a child, depending on him alone to accept you, just as you are.

Dear precious Father,

Help me to truly understand and know your compassionate love for me. Help me to quiet my heart and lean against you as a small baby leans against her mother. Please open my eyes to your priorities, and give me eyes in my heart to see you and enjoy you each day. I do love you! In Jesus' name, amen.

Ten

Listening for the Music of God's Voice

I have always been a romanticist. Perhaps most women are. I love the stories of the prince coming on his white horse to rescue his fair princess. The two fall deeply in love, get married, rule over their kingdom together, and live happily ever after. As a young girl, my heart filled with anticipation and excitement as I dreamed about my own prince coming for me someday.

In all of these stories, the princess engages her heart to her prince, and she follows him in utter devotion. These longings and dreams are so universal throughout history and through every culture that it must be a pattern for what we were created to experience in the beginning, before the fall of man. In other words these stories are a remnant of what God originally created life to be. I think each woman was made to be loved deeply and to feel connected to another with whom she can partner in life and make a mark. We were made for love and to have meaning in our lives.

In a fallen world, where sin, death, and darkness have marred and hidden so many truths that God originally created us to know, we must look for the original patterns and follow diligently after them. I believe the reason so many are captivated by epic stories is because we were made to be a part of great adventure, divine beauty, and magnificent love. In contemporary life, fans are captivated by movies like *The Lord of the Rings; The Lion, the Witch and the Wardrobe; Star Wars;* and many more in which good and evil battle for the soul and well-being of a kingdom or people. These stories satisfy a deep place in our hearts, as the protagonists or heroes fight with all their might against evil and great odds and ultimately conquer. The ends of these stories give hope and a pattern of heroism for those of us who long to be part of a grand adventure, who long to live courageously.

Yet these are merely shadows of the biggest and truest epic narrative. The story begins with a great king, our Creator, who made us for his pleasure, giving us a beautiful kingdom in which to live, love, and enjoy life. But a wicked enemy, Satan, comes along, jealously wanting to undermine the loyalty of the King's own children. He deceives them with lies about their King and captures their allegiance. He takes them to his kingdom of darkness to serve him. Yet the righteous King, being noble and perfect in his love, does everything in his power to win back and redeem his lost children—to retrieve them from a kingdom of darkness and bring them home to the kingdom of light, for which they were created. Doing so costs the King the life of his Son, but no sacrifice is too great to bring his children back into his realm.

And so the greatest Prince, Jesus, gave himself so that we might live again with the King. But this noble Prince had power even over death and was raised from a brutal death to celebrate life and be with his beloved children for all eternity.

If we really believed and understood that this is the *true* story of our lives, then we would look with hope, courage, and deep devotion for the day when all of us will be rescued from this realm of darkness and be restored into his presence. We would also understand that our part in the battle is strategic. Each of us has the ability to bring light, love, beauty, and his presence into every place we go. The interesting thing is that this kingdom of light, though invisible and mysterious and somewhat hidden in this world, already exists today in the spiritual realm. And our King, who is ultimately going to redeem us, is alive and active in our lives and in this world *today.*

As I have pondered just what it means for me to dance in a manner worthy of my heavenly King, I've learned that my heart must be fully engaged with his, as the princess's heart was engaged with the prince in all the stories I treasured as a girl. Delighting in his presence; admiring his strength and integrity; resting in the security and protection of his love and commitment. The state of a girl's heart reveals the quality of her love and devotion for her king.

In studying biblical joy through all the concepts shared in this book, I have become more and more convinced that dancing well requires just such a devoted heart. Joy is not found in doing—"If I follow this formula and do enough good work, then I will find joy." It is not dependent on our deserving—"If I am good enough and do righteous acts, then God will reveal his joy to me." It is not secured by acquiring things or getting all that we want—"If my husband changes, and we have a better salary, or my child is healed, then I will have joy."

Joy is established in the secret places of our heart, where we receive the love of our King and love him back. It is our heart that determines our joy. How important it is, then, that we diligently guard our heart and protect it from the attack of the one who would have us doubt our great King.

Be glad of life because it gives you the chance to love
and to work and to play and to look up at the stars.

Henry Van Dyke

How the Secret Garden Grows

This concept of protecting the greatest treasure of my life, my heart, became clear to me on the last couple days of my vacation in England, which I mentioned earlier. This particular morning was one of those delightful times when life seems more like a storybook than reality. After sipping steaming hot tea from china mugs and satiating our hunger with a full, traditional English breakfast of fried eggs, bacon, toast, jam, tomatoes, and baked beans in our little cottage bed-and-breakfast, we were ready for a day of adventure. My two daughters, a close friend, and I were two days from flying back to America after our glorious week of tromping through towns all over northern England, so we were savoring each precious moment.

Exploring the hometown of James Herriot was our first goal on this day. He was the British veterinarian whose stories of his ventures into the Yorkshire dells have delighted thousands of people. We ventured out onto gray cobblestone streets. Cottages that appeared as dollhouses lined winding lanes. Even in October, the gardens surrounding the cottages were in full bloom with tall red rosebushes clinging to the walls of the houses, sunflowers swaying in the breeze, and rhododendrons still blooming in proliferation.

A local bus ride to another small town featuring castle ruins and a famous teahouse promised a fitting end to a memorable day. Climbing up several stairs to sit on the second tier of the bus provided us with wonderful views of the countryside landscape. Broad fields of grass and farmland surrounded us on both sides as we bumped up and down the narrow, winding roads.

Most interesting, though, were the gigantic hedges. In other places we had traveled, wire fences or stone walls separated one piece of property from another. But here, tall hedges separated one farm from another.

The hedges were very thick from top to bottom. Some were as much as twelve feet high and three to four feet wide. These were literally walls made of dense bushes! I had always heard the phrase "hedge of protection," but now I knew what it meant. A tall, thick, dense hedge provides a wall of protection around a farmer's property—to keep unwanted animals out and to shelter the fields and animals inside his property from harm.

We arrived in a thriving village that dated back to the twelfth century. Ruins of a convent bordered the edge of town. Seems that Henry VIII had all the convents destroyed when he separated England from the Roman Catholic Church, so all that was left of what had been a beautiful cathedral was a magnificent wall and outer structure.

We wandered down narrow lanes and were deeply delighted with a profusion of blooming flowers. At the end of one tiny street, a circular hedge towered above our heads, with sunflowers peeping over the top. Just then, a rosy-cheeked elderly woman came out of a gate in the middle of the hedge. She smiled cheerily as she caught us straining to get a glimpse of what was inside.

"Come see my garden," she said. We peered through the gate like little girls in a candy shop. The garden was quintessentially English. Most spectacular were bushes aflame with roses of pink, red, yellow, and coral—several of which were climbing the old wall of her house. A variety of other flowers burst forth with so many colors I could barely count them all. Evident was the skill and design of an artist who had planned and cultivated each area to perfection.

"This is my artwork," she told us. "The secret to a beautiful garden is to choose the plants that you want to grow and plant them carefully. Next, you must ensure that they receive lots of fertilizer, water, and sunshine—as it takes lots of work to see that the right plants grow. Then the master gardener must watch over them, nurture them, protect them.

Whatever one waters will grow. Whatever one neglects will surely die. All pesky weeds must be picked—and one must be vigilant about this task."

She pointed over to the hedge.

"Finally, I have surrounded the borders of my garden with a protective hedge to keep any animals, winds, or other harmful varmints from getting in to destroy the plants I have so purposefully planted. I am very intentional about my garden, and it has provided me with many years of pure joy. All gardens are prone toward ruin unless they are cared for every day. But mine is a work of love, and so I am committed to keeping it beautiful every day, as long as I live."

> Watch over your heart with all diligence,
> for from it flow the springs of life.
>
> PROVERBS 4:23

GARDENING OUR OWN HEARTS

Later, as we rode the bus back to our bed-and-breakfast, I considered what this sweet elderly woman had said. The picture of my own heart as a garden of life came into my mind. I remembered the verse, "Watch over your heart with all diligence, for from it flow the springs of life" (Proverbs 4:23). My heart is the wellspring from which all the rest of my life is conducted. I must choose what thoughts, convictions, ideas, and beliefs to plant so that my heart will continue to grow into a beautiful haven in which I can worship God.

As the elderly gardener was intentional about what she planted, so I must be intentional. I must water and feed those things that I want to grow. If I want to grow a heart of joy, then I must plant the words of God and his truth. I must feed joy daily to ensure that it becomes a healthy fruit of my heart. I must be vigilant to pick and demolish the weeds of doubt, despair, sin, complaint, and selfishness, which threaten to overcome this joy. A hedge of protection should be in place so that nothing comes in to destroy the very place that God designed for me to cultivate faith, truth, beauty, and joy.

One of the most vital truths I learned from my gardener friend is that it takes diligence and constant vigilance to ensure that a garden remains healthy, vigorous, and strong. It requires attentive care, every day. "All gardens are prone toward ruin unless they are cared for every day," she said "But mine is a work of love, and so I am committed to keeping it beautiful as long as I live." These words of hers live on in my thoughts and dovetail with the proverb, "Watch over your heart with all diligence." Diligence definitely needs to be a resolve and commitment so that nothing robs me of the fruit of joy.

Even as the old woman worked and watched over her garden every day, so I need to prune and protect, water and weed daily if I want my devotion and pure love for God to blossom and grow. In doing so, the garden of my heart becomes a work of art for God's glory.

When I returned home, I talked to my husband about this image. He told me he had once done a study of Proverbs 4:23. He discovered that the meaning of the words in the original Hebrew referred to watching over and protecting the borders and boundaries of your heart—much as a farmer guards and protects the borders of his farm. The concept inferred that we must be careful about what is allowed into the borders of the land, to be sure it is held safe, protected, and ultimately productive.

Through delving into the concepts covered in the previous chapters, I have realized that everything about joy is related to the condition of my heart: truly, if I am going to walk in a life of joy, my heart needs to be planted in the soil of God's Word, watered and fertilized with the continual reading, praying, and exercising of faith; protected and weeded from all doubt, despair, and lies; and guarded against the onslaught of the Enemy. This requires that I make decisions every moment to trust in the Holy Spirit, to seek to please him, so that he will not be quenched.

This whole concept of gardening helped me to understand what I need to do to keep a heart ready to dance with my Lord, fully engaged in love, and prepared to follow his lead and instruction as we move through daily life, partners unified in each step.

> Your words were found and I ate them, and Your words
> became for me a joy and the delight of my heart; for
> I have been called by Your name, O LORD God of hosts.
>
> JEREMIAH 15:16

PLANTING THE SEED OF GOD'S WORD

God has desired from the beginning to be intimately involved in the lives of his children. Loving them, providing for them, protecting them, and communing with them is the very essence of his personality. Even in Genesis, we see him walking in the garden he made for Adam and Eve, wanting to talk with them, to be with them. God likes to talk! He is a communicator. Nothing draws me closer to a friend than to be able to share my thoughts and ideas, and to be understood, validated, and loved in return—and that's the kind of intimacy God wants to share with me.

My Father longs to talk to me and to have me listen, to delight in his words and to respond. He has so eloquently provided us with a means of knowing his heart by giving us his words in Scripture. The Old Testament prophet Jeremiah talked of eating it: "Your words were found and I ate them, and Your words became for me a joy and the delight of my heart; for I have been called by Your name, O LORD God of hosts" (Jeremiah 15:16).

Jeremiah painted a picture of taking the Lord's words inside of his very being, digesting them, cherishing them, allowing them to be woven into the fabric of his being. This verse, though, also links God's words to our hearts: they "became for me a joy and delight of my heart." God's words are true, pure, and sure—and they bring joy! Joy because, as the verse says, "I have been called by Your name!" I am his family; he is mine, we are his. We are connected eternally to him.

How amazingly Jeremiah put his finger on the source of our joy: hearing, knowing, digesting, living by God's words of truth, comfort, guidance, love, and grace. God wants us to have his assurance and hear his voice every day, *every minute*—even as Satan would love for us to doubt and not hear his words.

In order to have God's words living in my heart, I must make time every day, to store them there. I must build up a reservoir of his communication to me so that I will be able to draw at any moment from this storehouse of his words. The more time I spend with him in Scripture, the more vocabulary the Holy Spirit will have to speak to me through each moment.

Busyness and the constant stresses of life rob me of physical, emotional, and spiritual strength. Even as I must restore myself physically every day, sleeping and eating in order to give my body the nutrients and strength it needs to live productively, so I must feed my soul on God's Word, nurture my heart through prayer, and pull away from life's demands in order to rest. The more active I am and the more responsibility

I have, the more I will be taxed. The only way I will be able to experience his presence and know his words is to *make time* for him. My joy is essentially dependent on my scheduling time to hear his Word, to place it into the very body of my life as Jeremiah suggests. His Word will follow me, whisper in my ear, encourage my heart, guide my way, protect me from deception, but *only* if I have made time to hear it.

The habit of meeting with God every day was modeled for me as a young Christian. I had a friend a few years older than me who would light a candle in her apartment, brew a hot cup of tea or apple cider, and invite me to join her in studying the Word. "Let's spend time together listening to what God has to tell us today," she invited in her soothing, assuring voice. I so enjoyed her friendship, and I learned to love God's friendship in such a context. Making time almost every morning to continue this habit has become an essential lifeline for me.

SPIRITUAL EARPLUGS

As I tried to get to the root of my own discouragement and weariness, I unearthed another factor: the messages of false thinking that surround me everywhere. I hear these messages in the media—on television and in advertisements—from colleagues, and also from within. Often these messages are disguised as voices of fear. *What if the financial issues affect our ministry and we are not able to make the payment on our house? What will we do to make a living? What if my son doesn't get a job soon and his school debt comes due? Will my child make it through the challenges of adolescence with her morality intact? What about my daughter's health issues—what if they're serious?*

Lies are all around me, suggesting that God will not answer prayer or that I don't deserve his response because of my own imperfections.

Sometimes critical thoughts or petty jealousy or irritation can separate me from people. My own selfishness or sin can shout loudly and distract me from hearing his voice. *I do all the work, and no one appreciates me. I think so-and-so doesn't like me. Such and such isn't fair—I shouldn't have to deal with this issue. Can I really believe that God will work in this situation? It looks pretty beyond his control to me.* Over and over the voices bombard my mind and heart.

This is why the Word of God is compared to a sword of the Holy Spirit (Ephesians 6:17). If we listen to God's voice by reading Scripture and talking with him every day through prayer, we store up a reservoir of truth that the Holy Spirit, God in us, can then use. He will speak into the battles of our lives to fight against all that would seek to destroy his truth and beauty.

Learning how to listen for God's voice amid the noise of life and the lies of the Enemy is essential to remaining in his joy. A few years ago, my family and I moved to a new city. We rented a house to stay in until we could find a home suitable for our family of six. My older teenagers' rooms were right on top of my bedroom. I am a light sleeper, and so every night, when they would stay up later than I or come in late from meeting with a friend or working, I would be awakened. I could hear them brush their teeth, take showers, talk to each other. So I started using earplugs. I was amazed at how little noise I heard when I stuffed my ears with tiny little rubber stoppers! I could finally sleep soundly because all the racket had gone away.

As I became aware of all the voices filled with false messages, I realized that I needed to develop spiritual earplugs. I needed to silence the voice of Satan and the noise of other messages that deplete me so that I could hear only God's voice informing my mind and heart. When I resolved to listen only to God's voice and truth, I began to develop a habit that grows stronger each day: I'm better able to recognize the true voice, and I capture all the other thoughts and voices and pluck them out of my mind.

Paul taught us, "We are destroying speculations and every lofty thing raised up against the knowledge of God, and we are taking every thought captive to the obedience of Christ" (2 Corinthians 10:5).

What a great picture this is for me: I am destroying—totally killing and getting rid of—*any* thought raised against the truth of God. I *can* take every thought as a captive, a prisoner, to the obedience of Christ. Here, again, I am reminded of a garden. I picture diligently guarding the borders of my mind, keeping all the bad varmints away and protecting the garden of my thoughts within. If I allow a weed of a thought into my mind and then water it, it will grow! I need to be aware of what thoughts I encourage to grow. Any thoughts of despair, fear, or falsehood that arise against the words of God need to be immediately dealt with and destroyed. I can dispatch them promptly when I cherish God's voice, when I listen to his words, memorize them, and repeat them. They are water for the garden of my soul. They become the lyrics of the song to which my Father and I dance the best.

The great teachings unanimously emphasize that all the peace, wisdom, and joy in the universe are already within us; we don't have to gain, develop, or attain them. We're like a child standing in a beautiful park with his eyes shut tight. We don't need to imagine trees, flowers, deer, birds, and sky; we merely need to open our eyes and realize what is already here, who we really are—as soon as we quit pretending we're small or unholy.

UNKNOWN

The Oil of Joy

God my Father longs for intimacy with me because he is relational. It is why he became one of us, not far off but close and personal. It is why he became a man, Jesus, who laughed and touched and healed and cried.

If I want to dance more closely with my Father, I need only to look at Jesus to fall in love with him more. Hebrews 1:9 says of him, "You have loved righteousness and hated wickedness; therefore God, your God, has set you above your companions by anointing you with the oil of joy" (NIV). Ultimately, Jesus was joyful, by God's own design and anointing. He was anointed to fulfill his purpose on the earth: to redeem those who were far from God. That's a joyful purpose! Therefore, Jesus is our ultimate model of joy incarnate. The way he lived humbly among people; the way he reached out to those who were needy; the way he saw worth in women and children and tax collectors and fishermen. A man of joy who slept in a storm because of his confidence in the Father. The One who taught through the picture of nature, telling his disciples to notice the lilies of the field and used fig trees.

Another place in the Bible talks about Jesus' anointing: Isaiah 61:1–3 also draws attention to Jesus' purpose of bringing joy, redemption, and freedom.

> The Spirit of the Lord GOD is upon me,
> Because the LORD has *anointed* me
> To bring good news to the afflicted;
> He has sent me to bind up the brokenhearted,
> To proclaim liberty to captives
> And freedom to prisoners;
> To proclaim the favorable year of the LORD
> And the day of vengeance of our God;

To comfort all who mourn...
Giving them a garland instead of ashes,
The oil of gladness instead of mourning,
The mantle of praise instead of a spirit of fainting
So they will be called oaks of righteousness,
The planting of the LORD, that He may be glorified.

So joy is intricately woven into restoration and hope; the spirit of joy compelled Jesus to give, serve, love, restore hope, and comfort those who mourn. The oil of gladness of the Lord is the resource of living waters that come from experiencing for ourselves his gentleness and comfort.

In Matthew 11:29, Jesus said, "Take My yoke upon you and *learn from Me,* for I am gentle and humble in heart, and you will find rest for your souls." It is this phrase that has stuck in my mind: *learn from me.* He lived a life of humbleness and gentleness. If I live the way he lived, I will find the deep down, bubbling over, satisfying joy that God created me to have. If Jesus didn't need all the trappings of this world—possessions, fame, acceptance, a degree—and *he* was joyful, then seeking him, loving him, knowing him, and modeling him will be my ultimate source of joy.

In the past couple of years, I have realized that it is as I ponder Jesus—think about him, study him, read about him, model him—that my life becomes more fully what it is supposed to be in all areas. Jesus is the ultimate portrait of living with joy. But even more, I have sought to understand what it means to love him with my whole heart, as he so desires. If Jesus, the man anointed with the oil of joy and gladness, was about serving others to the point of laying down his life for them, then serving others and giving myself to the cause of Christ must be the place in which I will find joy.

I experienced this firsthand many years ago. I was pregnant with what I thought was my fourth child. About fourteen weeks into the pregnancy I began to hemorrhage. We had recently moved to a new area, and

I didn't have a doctor yet. I became so weak I could only lie in our bathtub. The bleeding was so profuse that I passed out. As Clay tried to care for me, one of my children called a neighbor for help, who then called a midwife she knew.

After what seemed like hours, a quiet, gentle woman came into the bathroom. I could barely lift my head to see her clearly.

She said very gently, "Sally, my name is Heather, and I'm here to help you and comfort you. Don't worry. We'll get you the help you need. Just rest in my arms." Then she bent down to me, in all my gore, and touched my head. She pushed my hair out of my face, held me up with one hand under my neck, and began to wash away the blood. She spoke soft words of reassurance and breathed quiet, whispered prayers as she took care of me and asked me medical questions. An incredible peace touched my soul and gave me the assurance that I was not alone but that God was right there, caring for me, loving me, comforting me. She ushered the very presence of Jesus into that tiny bathroom.

Though I was eventually rushed to the hospital by ambulance in an emergency effort to save my life, I still remember this event as one in which I felt more love than I remember feeling in almost my whole life. God's Spirit touched me in a deep place in my heart and gave me peace. It seemed so illogical that anyone would be put upon to touch me in my messy state, and yet in the midst of the chaos, God, through his obedient servant, touched me and brought me his hope and transcendent joy. He was there, he cared, and he touched and loved me in a tangible way.

God's voice speaking peace is the
sweetest music an ear can hear.

Charles Haddon Spurgeon

PRACTICING THE DANCE

When a maiden takes the hand of her lover and dances with him, her heart is filled with love, appreciation, and admiration for him. Their dance becomes one of beauty, grace, and unity. The more the partners dance together, the more elegant the steps, and the more the dancers learn to respond to each movement and gesture of their partner.

For my own heart to be so engaged in the dance with my loving heavenly Father, I must come with a heart filled with love for him, appreciative of his wonderful qualities, and responsive to his strength and grace to lead me. And I dance with the joy he created me to experience.

I remember with gladness of heart the passage in Psalm 30:11–12, in which God speaks to us of the joy he will bring to us as we hold his hand:

> You have turned for me my mourning into dancing;
> You have loosed my sackcloth and girded me with gladness,
> That my soul may sing praise to You and not be silent.
> O LORD my God, I will give thanks to You forever.

I have asked God to show me the state of my "garden," so to speak. As I shine the light of his Word into my heart, I can see where there are weeds to pick. As I ponder his attributes and love in the stories about his love and faithfulness, I have sought to plant and water these treasures in the foundations of my heart. Just this action has better fitted me to be his dance partner. I know that he sees me for who I am, the person of my heart. He speaks his love to my soul, takes my hand, and dances with me in practice for the final dance when we will be in his presence forever and celebrate joy unconstrained.

Finding *Your* Rhythm in God's Joy

1. Proverbs 4:23 tells us to guard our hearts "with all diligence."
   Do a heart exam. Write down any thoughts, attitudes, or fears
   you need to remove. Put your finger on any attitudes that
   have been allowed to grow (hate, bitterness, pride, false ambi-
   tion, pettiness, etc.), which will cause your heart harm.

   Now commit your heart into God's hands and ask
   him to help you to be a wise gardener of your heart.

2. Jeremiah 15:16 shows us the importance of ingesting the
   words, thoughts, and intentions of God by studying his
   Word. What was the consequence in Jeremiah's life when
   he "ate the word"?

   Make a project of reading through one psalm a day and
   circle all of the attributes you see that belong to God.

3. Read Psalm 1.

> How blessed is the man who does not walk in the
>   counsel of the wicked,
> Nor stand in the path of sinners,
> Nor sit in the seat of scoffers!
> But his delight is in the law of the LORD,
> And in His law he meditates day and night.
> He will be like a tree firmly planted by streams of water,
> Which yields its fruit in its season
> And its leaf does not wither;
> And in whatever he does, he prospers.
>
> The wicked are not so,
> But they are like chaff which the wind drives away.
> Therefore the wicked will not stand in the judgment,
> Nor sinners in the assembly of the righteous.
> For the LORD knows the way of the righteous,
> But the way of the wicked will perish.

What does this passage say about the person who
meditates on God's Word? How often does this
"blessed man" think about God's Law?

What is a tree like that is watered by streams of water?
How does this apply to the person who delights in his
Word? When does this tree yield its fruit?

Evaluate your own practice of reading and meditating
on God's Word. Plan a realistic time for including
Bible reading into your current schedule.

4. According to Psalm 30:11–12, who has turned David's
   mourning into dancing?

What has God clothed David with?

Who ultimately is responsible to give you a heart of
joy and gladness?

Examine your life to see if you have been looking for things outside of your heart to provide you with a source of joy. Anything we depend on besides God is an idol. Identify any idols and determine to recognize them and rid your heart of them.

My precious Father,

How grateful I am that you are my King, my Redeemer. Open the eyes of my heart so that I may see the bigger picture of history, of which I can play a part. Help me to know you as my lover, my caretaker, my friend, and my king. Show me how to dance in your reality every day. Give me eyes to see the truth of your kingdom and prepare me for the celebration of life with you, which will go on through all eternity. Sweet Lord, restore to me the joy of my salvation. I love you so much. In Jesus, my Prince's name, I come. Amen.

Will You Join the Dance?

Now is the time for you to determine how you will dance through your life. God's desire is that we see him in all the days and places of our lives, hear his voice whispering to us each moment, and surrender to his Spirit who wants to fill our hearts with the fruit of his own joy.

He desires that all who observe us see a palpable life, energy, strength, peace, and childlike joy bubbling up from within us. It comes because of the secret hand that is guiding, loving, and dancing with us each step of the way. Those qualities are only a hand grasp away. Will you surrender your burdens and empty your hands so that his strong hand may lead and guide you to a place where he dwells and where he will turn your mourning into dancing?

Each of us must make a choice from our heart, before God. "No matter what my life holds, I will choose, with the eyes of my heart, to see your goodness, to trust you in all seasons of life, to seek to dance with you in the joy you have provided. I will choose to bring your light into the dark places of my life. I will, as Christ, for the joy before me in eternity, see things from an eternal perspective and recognize your hand of love in each moment of my life. I will sow seeds of faith hope and joy in the garden of my heart, so that I will reap a harvest of joy. As an act of my will, I will follow your lead from this day forward."

My hope is that more and more of us will learn the steps of his dance, that his reality may invade our world with light and beauty every day. May God bless you with joy in your dance as you are held in the arms of the Creator of beauty, love, and everlasting joy.

I pray that you and all who read this book will hear the following psalm echoed in the melody of your own heart:

Praise the LORD!
Sing to the LORD a new song,
And His praise in the congregation of the godly ones.
Let Israel be glad in his Maker;
Let the sons of Zion rejoice in their King.
Let them praise His name with dancing;
Let them sing praises to Him with timbrel and lyre.
For the LORD takes pleasure in His people;
He will beautify the afflicted ones with salvation.

Let the godly ones exult in glory;
Let them sing for joy on their beds...
This is an honor for all His godly ones.
Praise the LORD! (Psalm 149:1–5, 9)

God loves you so dearly and is waiting to show you the invisible hand of his love, his beauty, his blessing, and his joy each and every day of your life. May he keep us all dancing and loving and celebrating his reality until we see him face to face.

Sally Clarkson
June 2009

Notes

Chapter 3

1. L. M. Montgomery, *Rilla of Ingleside* (New York: Frederick A. Stokes, 1921), 250–51.

Chapter 9

1. Julian of Norwich, *Revelations of Divine Love,* ed. Grace Warrack (London: Methuens, 1901), 11.

Acknowledgments

Any of my books are always as a result of the many life-giving relationships I have experienced.

Clay, thanks for having the idea of making my little story into a book. You always inspire me to keep going and to write better books.

Sarah and Joy, I cherish you as my "girls' club" companions, and you are two of my greatest sources of joy.

Joel and Nathan, I am amazed at how much our friendship means to me and how much encouragement you have both given to me personally in the midst of busy lives.

Gwen, I love you for being my sister-friend through all the years.

Deb, Shelley, Lynn, Beth, Sandra, Micala, Lisa, Marla, Jerrine, Wendy, Tammie, Vickie, Michelle, Janet, Phyllis, Jossie, Holly, Stacy, Karla, Louella, Brandee, Brenda, Liz—you are my stalwart, loving, encouraging, always-keep-me-going friends. I love you and appreciate you forever. Without you, I would quit writing.

Laura Barker, my lovely editor, believed in the project and has borne with it patiently through all the computer glitches and time constraints. I appreciate you, Laura, and am so glad you are so gifted!

What a blessing it was to work with Ginger K.—a delightful new friend.

There are so many more who send me e-mails, surprise gifts, or cards, and all of you are what this book is about—the joy we share in the Lord as we live through this journey together. May his joy renew you and bless you every day.

About the Author

Sally Clarkson enjoys being a wife and mother of four and is a popular author, speaker, and teacher. Since 1975, she has ministered to Christian women and mothers nationally and internationally, traveling to more than a dozen countries. She and her husband, Clay, minister now full time through Whole Heart Ministries, which they founded in 1994 to strengthen Christian homes by "keeping faith in the family."

Sally is an inspiring author whose books include *Seasons of a Mother's Heart, The Mission of Motherhood, The Ministry of Motherhood,* and *The Mom Walk*. Her books have been translated into Dutch, French, Korean, and Chinese.

Sally speaks from her heart to the heart of Christian women out of a life of studying the Word and walking with God for more than thirty years. She also regularly encourages Christian women on her I Take Joy blog. Sally is a lover of good and beautiful books, strong English tea in a china cup, quiet walks on mountain trails, traveling and adventures, and baking her own whole wheat breads and rolls. She cherishes time with all her family, and especially treasures moments with her youngest daughter, Joy, who is her last child still at home and a fitting punctuation mark to the family.

For more information, you can reach her at:

Whole Heart Ministries

P.O. Box 3445

Monument, CO 80132

whm@wholeheart.org

www.wholeheart.org

www.itakejoy.com

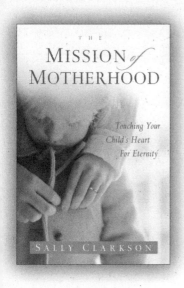

There is no greater, nobler, or more fulfilling calling than that of motherhood. Yet today's culture often minimizes that vital role, and women may not embrace that desire or calling with their whole hearts.

By catching a vision of God's original design and allowing it to shape their lives, mothers can rediscover the joy and fulfillment to be found in the strategic role to which God has called them—for a purpose far greater than they can imagine.

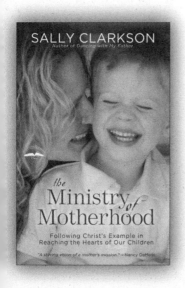

This inspiring book helps moms use each moment of their day to strategically pass on five gifts to their children: grace, inspiration, faith, training and service. *Ministry of Motherhood* will inspire and equip you to intentionally embrace the rewarding, desperately needed, and immeasurably valuable opportunities for spiritual nurture and training in your children's lives. Because motherhood isn't just a job; it's a calling.

WATERBROOK PRESS
www.waterbrookmultnomah.com